LIMITLESS

a guide to finding your greatest self

———

AMY
ARVARY

Amy Arvary Conscious Style
amyarvarycs.com

ISBN-13: 978-0692138717

This book is dedicated to my family, friends and clients who have lovingly supported and enriched this journey.

An extra special thanks to Lorraine, Chrissy and Jessica for helping to put it all together so beautifully.

CONTENTS

Introduction

In 2007, Amy Arvary began an extraordinary journey in and out of a darkness that catapulted her into a life that she never expected. Emerging from that dark period she stumbled upon new answers to old questions. The things she learned captivated her. Suddenly what she had always thought was true about her and the world around her began radically shifting

She was awakening.

As she dug deep into her own thoughts and behaviors, she learned to identify and let go of the thoughts that were no longer in alignment with what she wished for. This brought about changes that she and others began to notice.

Eagerly, she shared her new findings with everyone she could, and people started coming—with all kinds of issues for her to help guide them through. She was laying a path to the life she desired and wasn't even aware of it. As she built this ladder of assistance for others, she too found more and more relief from the pair that once took residence inside of her. She was manifesting, creating a new life, and began moving from what was, to what was becoming.

It has been over 10 years since that dark time. Ms. Arvary has helped people across the globe overcome, achieve, and attract what they desire. Limitless: a guide to finding your greatest self, answers the question she hears most often, "What is it that you actually do?" More importantly, this book will help guide you to the things that YOU desire using examples of real life stories and things you can begin doing right NOW that will help shift you into the lane you wish to be in.

Grab a pen. Get comfortable, and enjoy this journey you are about to embark upon.

You are ready. You have been preparing your whole life for this moment. This is your opportunity to discover what you are creating, what it is you are practicing, who it is you are becoming... who it is you are.

We are manifesting.

We are limitless.

CHAPTER ONE
where it began

When I was pregnant in 2005 I bought a journal. It was a pretty journal, pink with muted silver design. It was intended for my daughter who would be joining me soon.

I felt the bigness of becoming a mom immediately and thought how cool it would be if I could somehow pass to her my perspective on things. My hope was that one day she would be able to understand my motivations and reasonings for all of the things we were about to experience together. I thought this was brilliant. I would dedicate this journal to my daughter and share with her the details of our life together through my voice.

I imagined gifting it to her as an adult. I imagined how my perspective could shed light on whatever she may not have understood as a young child. I imagined it to be the perfect gift—a greater understanding of our personal world's whys and hows and whens.

There was just one problem. Every time I sat to write I would freeze. I was terrified to make a mark in the book. I was terrified that my handwriting would be too messy or that my spelling would be an embarrassment. I felt paralyzed with insecurity and fear. So I wouldn't.

So I didn't.

The following year I gave birth to my first, only and most perfect human being I know. My daughter was a gift and she changed my life immediately. Our first months together were a blur—a joyful and exhausting blur until one day, she sat up on her own and suddenly my love was greater than my fear. I found her journal. I took a deep breath and began our story.

What a story it has become.

"*Sunday April 9, 2006*

I bought this journal over a year ago—February, 2005. I bought this journal for you, Izabella. I bought it as a gift for you to be able to share with me all of our history together. I have attempted to begin writing but when I try to start writing, I get so nervous and stop. It has taken me over a year to get over my anxiety. I have been so nervous that I would say the wrong things at the wrong time and that I would appear to you as someone you do not admire and respect.

Over the past year, however, I have experienced things that I really wish I recorded for you to share with me.

This week you sat up all on your own and I decided I have to get over it because your life, our life together, has been such a precious gift that I need to share it with you regardless of my fear. So we begin. And just remember that I love you more than I ever knew was possible. Thank you..."

I didn't know it at the time but I was overcoming. I was overcoming a fear that I would have much preferred to ignore. Sharing my thoughts would leave me vulnerable. It would call to attention all that is wrong with me. The fear of not being perfect prevented me from even believing I could be good—at anything.

I have come to understand that the best way to see something clearly is through the lens of hindsight. Have you ever noticed that? How many times have you walked away from someone saying, " I should have said…"? How many times have you discovered information about something that changed the way you once saw it? On the flip side of that, have you ever tried something new and discovered it wasn't what you had thought? We seem to try to force things, to know things, to judge things, all before we possibly can.

So I ask, why do we spend so much time thinking about the things we do in a way that prevents them from being what we wish or how we wish?

In my personal and professional life I have lived, learned and witnessed the effects that our thoughts have on us. Our thoughts are responsible for how we feel and how we behave. Our thoughts are responsible for the things we decide to take part in and the things we avoid. All of our fears and worries, all of our joys and successes—all of what we know stems from what we think of and how we think of it. And what is really important to know is that:

How you think has NOTHING to do with what's presently happening around you.

Being positive has nothing to do with circumstances.

I didn't know this for a very long time. As a matter of fact I didn't even begin questioning how I thought until my late 30's. Until then everything that happened in my life wasn't my fault or was. Sometimes I'd wake up and have a good day, sometimes id wake up and everything would be awful. In my mind I had a tremendous list of all the things wrong with me and a wonderfully detailed list of all the reasons why I could never, or would never, fill in the blank.

And this was ok because I wasn't even aware of it. I believed all of the stuff I told myself. They were my beliefs, my truths. I was certain about them. Every insecurity, every imitation, every fear—they were real. So real that they helped shape my life. So real I allowed myself to be held captive by them.

Until I didn't.

In 2007 life shifted greatly. At the time it seemed terrifying. Everything I once had was gone. Everything I once believed didn't make sense anymore. My world seemed to stop and for almost two years I struggled. I wanted to take my own life because I couldn't see beyond the failures and embarrassments. Without everything I believed to have once valued how could I possibly carry on?

The thoughts in my head fought with each other all day:

Take your life.

You are a failure.

You are an embarrassment.

You can't do this.

You are so stupid.

Look how FAT you are.

BUT...

you can't take your life because you have a daughter.

That's all I really had to prevent my suicide. My daughter. I had no idea how I would overcome that dark time but knew that having her grow up thinking that I didn't care enough to fight for our life together was not an option.

I didn't know it at the time but magic was happening and this shift was greater than I could have ever expected.

It had been almost two years. I sat with tears in my eyes and Xanax in my throat waiting for the pizza delivery man to arrive. I had gained over 100lbs—mostly pizza, wings and Xanax. The driver knew where he was going.

I had come home early because Oprah was having a show that I felt compelled to be home and watch. The show was about a woman who wrote a best selling book called The Secret. Oprah said that on this show they would be revealing the secret to life's happiness. I prepared myself to be healed.

The guest author, Rhonda Byrne, seemed so insightful.

Oprah seemed so interested. But the show ended and I sat on the couch confused. What the hell was the "secret"? How the hell did I miss it? This was my big chance to get out of the hell I was living... and I missed it. I missed the friggin' secret.

I could have dug deeper but truth is that I felt too sorry for myself. I was so angry and frustrated and sad... Hopeless, I was struggling to stay afloat.

Several months later some friends put a girls night together to get me out of the house...We joined at one of their homes and the host showed us a bunch of movies she had rented—all kinds, a big stack. In the middle of the stack I saw **The Secret**. I told the girls about Oprah and how I missed what the secret was and that I really wanted to see what it was all about so we watched it.

The lights went out and I must admit I was immediately PULLED into the movie. It was not like anything I had ever seen before. It was telling me things that I don't ever remember hearing. It spoke to me. It said, "Wake up AMY. You have the power to make this however you choose."

That was the beginning of what I refer to as my awakening. It really felt like I had come alive again...but in a very different way. The lights went on and I felt something besides sadness inside of me. It was like I was living in darkness but saw a glimmer of light.

I bought the DVD. I bought the CD. I played the DVD every second that my daughter wasn't watching Sesame Street. I listened to the CD every time I was in the car. I invaded my senses with this new material.

Not long after, I remember leaving for work with my daughter early in the morning. It had just started to rain. I looked at her and said, " today is a great day." As soon as I said it I was curious about how I could say such a thing. It was raining. I wanted to die. How could it be a great day?

As a matter of fact, I hadn't had a good day in almost two years. How could one rainy morning be a great day? This made me hungry—less for pizza this time and more for information. I needed to know what was going on in my brain that I could even think about having a good day.

I began studying the Thought Leaders in The Secret. Each one of them had a unique experience with changing their lives using some seemingly basic tools. I started with Bob Proctor and then studied one by one, Michael Bernard Beckwith, John Asseraff, Joe Vitale, Jack Canfield, Lisa Nicholas, Bill Harris, and John Demartini.

During that time I began researching the brain and how people feel better. I was shocked by this information I once knew nothing about. All of my searches led me to hypnosis. I will tell you that I had no interest in hypnosis. I wanted to know about my brain and how it worked. Still, my searches led to hypnosis.

I decided to see what it was all about. I didn't know anything about it. I remember it being a Wednesday because when I called the first place I saw online I remember the man on the phone telling me they only offered the intro class once a year and it started that coming Saturday. He said there was one seat available. I think I started crying then... I believed that seat was mine.

I told my boss in the salon I wanted to get this certification. I am forever grateful as she loaned me the $800 to begin, and I did 3 days later.

The day came and I arrived at the class early. I sat in my car across the street asking myself what the hell I was doing. How was I going to tell people I was going to do hypnosis? They would surely think I've lost my mind and yet I felt a pull... so I went inside, sat down and began learning. Right there, everything changed for me.

I learned about how we think. I learned about how we are programmed in our thinking since birth. I learned about self talk. I learned about letting go. I learned about the limitlessness of who we are and how we are. I learned about how we gather, interpret and store experiences. I learned about how our brains connect feelings with images. I learned so many things, so many helpful things.

I finished that certification quickly and immediately began the advanced certification. In the salon I set up in what was called the "quiet room". It was a small room that clients could rest between their spa services. I would practice there, relaxing them and getting comfortable with sharing this new skill.

I finished the advanced certification and moved right into a Masters Certification in Clinical Hypnotherapy. This stuff was life changing.

One day I was in the salon working with a client—a hair client—and the receptionist came to me and said, "Amy, there is a woman on the phone that wants to schedule an appointment with you for what you did when she was here for her facial." I couldn't believe it. Someone wanted an appointment for me to do hypnosis.

She took that appointment and I went to my boss again asking this time for some space in the salon to take clients for this service. I needed an office.

Downstairs, in the basement of the salon next to the laundry room, I cleared out the storage closet and set up shop. That was my first office. I studied like hell in there every second I wasn't on the floor working with a hair client. And clients started coming... and I was amazed with what was happening. Clients in pain both physically and emotionally would come and come back the following week lighter, freer, happier, more in balance. It was amazing.

After a couple of years I had acquired a nice office in a new salon. My time was divided between hair clients and hypnosis clients. When I didn't have a client I'd be reading or practicing on the hairdressers and spa ladies. I would practice on everyone. I was practicing on myself, trying everything I learned on me first then my friends then clients. Every day was different. I worked with clients suffering from depression, addiction, smoking, sex stuff, infertility, lupus, cancer, MS, test-taking, vertigo, stress, bereavement ... What I witnessed in that room was awesome.

CLIENT STORY

A regular client of one of the stylists in the salon approached me one day about helping her lose weight. Of course I said yes. At that time I had developed a very simple weight loss program. All the client had to do was show up once a week for our session, listen to our recording once a day and write down whatever she was thinking while she ate. I even gave her a notebook.

On our first visit, she explained to me that at 40 years old she was heavier that ever before. She told me that she had tried everything to lose weight and that the only reason she hadn't gotten surgery is because she was too heavy and at risk. She cried.

I explained that all she had to do was listen and write down what she's thinking while she eats—without any judgment, in her notebook. She left hopeful and excited.

The following week she came back and to my surprise she hadn't written anything in the notebook. I could tell she was embarrassed and feeling terribly guilty about it. She cried. I explained that if she didn't follow the program I couldn't continue to work with her. She agreed to do her part...

The following week she came back. This time she just cried. She hadn't filled out one word in her notebook. I couldn't believe it. I remember being so curious about how she could sincerely feel such desperation to lose weight but incapable of taking even just a simple step like writing down some words in a notebook. I believed she really wanted to lose weight. I also believed that she was stuck on something that was preventing her from losing the weight. It was clear that she had no idea what it could be.

That was the first time I ever suggested to do a life regression. I thought that if she could see her life as a progression of experiences each affecting each other that perhaps we could find where the block is. She was game.

With the lights dimmed and Zen garden playing on Pandora I relaxed her mind. I gave her an opportunity to go inside and make sense of things… I asked her to go to the last time she felt the most beautiful. I took her back further and further… then brought her back to present day.

She woke with a beautiful excitement recalling a time in her 20's that she was traveling for business and ran into an old friend at the airport. She told me that when he saw her he spun her around and with her skirt and hair it looked like something from a movie. She said, "I felt so beautiful". Then her face twisted up a bit as she said, "strange that my best day was also my worst day". When I asked her what she meant she told me that when she arrived in DC that evening she was raped in her hotel room.

WHAT? Yep. The day she felt her most beautiful was the day she was raped. Wonder why its difficult for her to lose weight and feel beautiful again? Now, she had been aware of the rape, even saw a counselor afterward. What she never realized was the connection in her thoughts that took place.

The following week she showed up with sneakers on, hopping up the stairs to my office with pep. She was down 8 pounds and brought with her a notebook filled with everything she was learning to let go of.

It has been 10 years since that time. I had changed so many things in my life. I became aware of everything I thought and everything I said. I feverishly tested new ideas that were coming my way and I pushed myself out of all of the limitations I was discovering that I had buried myself under....and as I did my world continued to shift. I continued to feel better. I began attracting new opportunities, new relationships.

The friends I once had began to fade out of picture as I became more clear about how I wanted to be behaving. The language I spoke changed. I found myself using words like "quantum physics" and "law of attraction" and "Manifesting" and "Source" and "programming". It was all so new and so, dare I say, magical.

Hypnosis led to letting go of my fears which led to changing my whole life. Each part was so necessary. Tracing it, had I not been depressed I wouldn't have looked for help and if I hadn't felt broken I wouldn't be here sharing this story. It is all so significant and brilliant—every moment, all of it. Like a song that I had been making without knowing it—each part a note that when put together constructed the most beautiful song I have never before heard and it was mine. It was my song.

REFLECTIONS

1. What are some of the things you wish you could change in your life?

_____

_____

_____

_____

_____

_____

_____

2. What are the things most important to you?

_____

_____

_____

_____

_____

_____

_____

3. What do you wish?

_____

_____

_____

_____

_____

_____

_____

_____

One of these things I've learned through my experience is that how we think about things greatly affects them. Although I may have heard that throughout my life, the meaning of that statement now holds a greater significance. In my experience, there are a few mindset shifts that have changed so much about the world I live in today.

The following are some of the most significant shifts that have occurred during my practice.

CHAPTER TWO

the RIGHT vs. WRONG mindset

We are taught from birth what is right and what is wrong. It is quite important to have those guidelines as we grow. The problem is that most of what we learn as right and wrong comes from sources that we have no control over. Our parents, our teachers, everyone, actually—they were all taught certain things by certain people too, and all of those people were taught certain things by people who all have their very own views and beliefs about the world.

As we evolve and begin understanding the world as adults, some of those truths don't feel right. Perhaps some of those rights don't feel so right to you. Maybe some of the wrongs don't actually seem wrong.

Then what?

We can choose to investigate why it doesn't feel right, or we can continue building our lives with those handed down beliefs.

There is a great story I heard along my way that really made me think about this. I have many but this one is one of my favorites…

A newly married wife was preparing a roast for her husband. He noticed she cut off the ends of the roast before putting it into the pan.

"Why did you cut the ends of the roast?" he asked his wife.

"That's how you make a roast," she replied.

This made him quite curious and when the holiday rolled around they were at her sister's house. She happened to be making a roast. The husband made sure to be in the kitchen to watch. Lo and behold she too cut the ends off the roast and put it in the pan! He couldn't believe it!

He said, "You do it too? Why do you cut the ends off the roast?"

She replied confidently, "That's how you make a roast."

Well the day came that they went to his mother-in-law's house. He got there early to get a good spot in the kitchen.

He watched as she gingerly took out the roast… and put it in the pan.

"Wait!" he yelled instinctively, "You forgot to cut the ends off!"

She turned and looked at him confused. "What are you talking about?" she asked.

"Both of your daughters told me that when you make a roast you have to cut the ends off before putting it in the pan. They said they learned it from you."

She smiled as she placed the pan on the counter and looked at him. "When the girls were young I didn't have a pan big enough to fit the roast."

Funny right? Not so much. It demonstrates exactly how we take what we are exposed to as truth—even without knowing the facts. That seems pretty dangerous to me.

But how many of us are living off of someone else's truths about who we are and the world around us? I certainly was and odds are good that there is still some of that in my programming. That's what makes it a practice. You must remember that you are manifesting, actively creating your life experience so adjust what is needed. Learn something new. Go somewhere new. Meet someone new. Stretch. Evolve. Let go of your fear.

Stop judging yourself and defending yourself.

Stop feeling guilty and stop feeling limited.

Your world is changing right this very moment. It has been since the moment you were born. Take a deep breath and feel it. Allow the oxygen around you to enter your body clearing out all stale energy…strengthening you and charging you and clearing you. Drop your shoulders as you exhale.

The outcomes in life are endless. We call them "possibilities," "expectations," "limitations," "restrictions," "mistakes," "accidents," "fate…"

Let go of what you think you know. Let go of what you see as right or wrong. Understand that people are doing the best they can at any given time based on what truths and beliefs they are operating from—just like you.

When I speak to groups, one of my favorite parts is right after the guided visualization. I am still so fascinated by how I can use words as simple as "meadow" or "energy" or "staircase" or "mountain" and everyone has a different image of that thing. It reminds me every time that what I say is triggering things in their personal experience, their "knowing." That's it. That's how we understand things, right? We get exposed to something—we see or hear, taste, touch or smell it and we decide something about it. Is it right or wrong? We base our answer on what we know. What we know is based on what we have already decided at some point in our lives and convinced ourselves to be true. But what if we don't have all of the information needed to fully or better understand what's happening?

We assume children can't understand everything adults do. We have ratings on movies and music protecting them from input that may be harmful in some way. We may behave differently in front of them by adjusting our language and behavior in some way. As an adult we can acknowledge that kids have much to learn about the world, and it's important they do so while growing; if they are interested in manifesting success of some kind.

But how many things did you decide when you were a kid? How much of what was happening in your world at that time wasn't what you actually thought? What if you only had some of the information, but as an adult it would make more sense or look different? How would that change things for you?

What if everyone didn't live like you did?

What if the people you thought had it good were suffering?

What if the things you once looked down upon become more understandable?

What if what you once thought of as right was suddenly wrong?

What if what you were made fun of was your superpower?

SHIFT

Many years ago I met a girl through a friend. She went to a different high school. My only real memory of her is that she hung out with what I considered a tough crowd and that she had a very bad reputation. She was called names like "slut" and well, you get it, I'm sure.

Almost 30 years later, our paths crossed. I came to learn that all during her middle and high school experience she was being sexually abused.

I couldn't believe it. I had no idea and if I had I certainly like to think I would have done something about it instead of just believing what everyone else said about her. I just didn't have the information and chose to believe what I did based on what I "heard."

I also remember growing up near a town that had a section which seemed to often have guys hanging out on the sidewalk. I remember learning they were always drunk. You could often see them stumbling down the street. I had even heard people getting so mad at them, that they would yell things like "You drunk!" and "loser" and things much worse.

Then one day, through a friend I met a super cool guy that was fighting a destructive disease. His nervous system was being destroyed and it was quickly removing his ability to control his body. He refused to go into the hospital even when he could barely balance himself to walk or do what most would consider easy daily tasks. He insisted on keeping his independence as the disease slowly took his life.

One day he told me that he didn't like to walk to town because people would throw things at him and call him a drunk when they drive by.

Oh, my heart. How could I have believed that those men in town were always drunk? Perhaps there was another truth, another reality—I just wasn't open to seeing it at the time.

I did the best I could with what I knew at the time. Just like today. Just like you, and just like everyone else. We are always simply working off of what we know until we know more or different.

That seems quite important now.

What is right and what is wrong?

What do you know, and what do you not know yet?

Does what you know help you to believe what you thought you knew or does it help support a successful version of what you desire to experience now?

When we get stuck on being right, we can't be open. Remember that what was once right may have shifted a bit. It may be time for you to loosen the grip and evolve your truths. You have been storing them in you since you were born.

Mental Exercise

Think about something in your life that is currently showing up a lot like money or relationships, weight or stress. It could be feelings of insecurity or fear, anger or hopelessness. Think about that thing in your life that takes up a lot of your time and energy.

Now think about how you think about it—What are those thoughts? What are the words you hear in your head when you imagine that thing?

Got that?

Now go back and see where you first remember that showing up in your life. When was the first time you learned about it or were exposed to it?

How old were you?

Now, with that information you can decide if those thoughts, those beliefs about that thing are in alignment with what you want now.

Oftentimes we can trace these experiences back to our childhood. However you felt and thought about it at that age, at that stage in your life, you stored it in you. From that moment on, that thought and those feels grew stronger and stronger becoming more and more true to you. You have probably even built your daily routine to include all of what you need to keep those beliefs still real to you because they are automatic.

Stopping to evaluate how you are thinking about things is important because **HOW WE THINK IS HOW WE MANIFEST.**

When what we use to believe clashes with what we need to believe to be in alignment with what we want, we get stuck in things like stress, frustration, anger and sadness, to name a few. We physically reject those old thoughts but never think to put new ones in.

Identify the thoughts and feelings that make you feel uncomfortable. See how you can use this exercise to check them.

Do they match with what you want? When you achieve that thing, will those thoughts be possible? Will they be helpful? If not, identify what thoughts and feelings WOULD be needed and practice them. Practice thinking and feeling that instead.

At one point in my life, right after I had my daughter, I remember driving down Route 80 near Parsippany, NJ. I specifically remember seeing an old, brown, rusty, pick up truck. It was driving next to me, in the middle lane as I was passing on the left. I remember thinking, "Who on earth would buy that car? I wonder, do people actually think, 'When I grow up I hope I get to have that beat up brown truck?" Who would choose that over these heated seats and comfort of my new car? Who would do that and why?"

I swear to you, I had no idea. It never dawned on me that money or circumstance helped shape that experience. It made no sense to me.

Not long after that, as everything around me crumbled, I found myself without a car. I was also without money. Through my darkness I couldn't see, but I was being taught such an important lesson. With my family's help I was able to get a car. It was a good car. It was a reliable car. No frills. No heated seats.

I'd like to say I learned a lesson and drove out of the lot giving thanks. That's not what happened. The truth is, I was in such a dark place—all I could see were the things that were gone. All I experienced was sadness, anger and guilt. As I drove out of the lot in a brand new car, I was angry. I was angry that I couldn't have what I wanted. I was sad that I needed help. And I hated that car. I hated how I sat in it—so erect, and I felt like a mom, like a single mom (whatever that meant to me at the time). It represented everything I couldn't once even understand.

It made me think about that brown pick up truck. It was the first time I ever realized people make decisions that they may not want to make. It made me see right and wrong so differently. It was at a time where everything that once seemed right wasn't, even when I tried really hard. Everything was different, and it scared the hell out of me.

I fought long and hard to get some of what once was back, but it was all gone.

I spent a long time in guilt, fear and shame. It's a dark place and the longer you stay the darker it gets. The moment I decided I couldn't take my own life, the practice of letting go became necessary. Letting go was critical. I had to let go of what was so that I could readjust my attention to what was becoming, even though I wasn't clear on that yet. I learned that THAT is where the power lies. I learned that letting go survives long after right and wrong. Letting go balances the contrast and adjusts the perspective accordingly. It allows you to move more fluidly to the thing you desire instead of the thing you fear.

Considering that we each believe only what we have convinced ourselves of, based on what we have experienced and how we have interpreted that experience, adjusting our thoughts is how we can expand our knowing. As much as this is true, I have come to understand that what I do know is that everything changes and evolves. Nothing stays the same, and there is more for me to learn about than the time I have to do so in this lifetime.

A right or wrong mindset is difficult to operate from with this understanding.

REFLECTIONS

1. What did you use to believe about:
MONEY

_____

_____

_____

_____

_____

_____

HEALTH

_____

_____

_____

_____

_____

_____

YOU

_____

_____

_____

_____

_____

_____

2. What would you LIKE to think about these topics:
MONEY

_____

_____

_____

_____

_____

HEALTH

_____

_____

_____

_____

_____

YOU

_____

_____

_____

_____

_____

CHAPTER THREE

WHAT WAS vs. WHAT IS vs. WHAT IS BECOMING mindset

As we grow, we come to understand our identity. We are given labels—stupid, smart, funny, lazy, athletic, serious, poor, rich, and so on. As we grow, we take these on as who we are. Someone else's opinion of us becomes our identity.

As we go through school we unknowingly reinforce those identities with our friends, our chosen activities and our interests. We attract those who are like what we think we are. But then we grow more, and as we grow we begin questioning some of those things we once believed. As we move into who we WANT to be, we may notice the things we no longer believe—about ourselves or the world.

The tricky part is that we grow believing these things about us and the world. When you begin the practice of manifesting these moments show up as frustration, fear, embarrassment and discomfort. You can actually feel it in your body. Did you ever receive upsetting news? Were you ever asked to participate in something that sounded great, but you talk yourself out of it? Do you carry the weight of lack or fear or worry or doubt? Where do you feel it in your body?

Close your eyes right now and think about that.

When you think of something that scares you where do you feel it in your body?

In my experience, oftentimes people feel it in either their stomach, chest or head. This is your body PHYSICALLY rejecting those automatic negative thoughts. They are actually hurting you, holding you back.

Once you become aware of your body's physical reaction to stress, you can use it as a tool to move beyond it. How? Well, once you become aware of that negative feeling you can, in that very moment, declare what you are thinking as void. It is no longer valid for the life you desire.

I recently received a phone call from a woman that I met at her therapist's office. I was called in to help her with some of the transitions she was trying to navigate. She was calling to tell me that something I said to her during that consultation resonated with her deeply, and that only a few days later she was already feeling so much freer and more alive.

During our consult, I told her that she could begin giving her brain a different program to work from. To do this, every time she heard herself say something in her head that was mean or limiting, she would practice catching that thought, pausing and replying with, "I can't believe I USED TO believe that." That's it. She had to just let her brain know that things are changing. Things are not what they use to be. Even if she's not clear on what she wants yet, she can use this to help loosen the grip on what was.

So she did it. I began seeing her shortly after. She was familiar with manifesting and was excited to adjust what was to better align with what was becoming. It was perfect for her.

Those old responses may no longer be in alignment with that thing you desire to feel or be or experience. Those negative thoughts can be holding you back, confining you in a box of lack and limitation—even if it isn't what you really want.

So, when you feel that feeling, take a deep breath and hold it for 5 seconds. Exhale slowly while dropping your shoulders. Repeat: "Thank you. Thank you. Thank you. Thank you."

Why "thank you?" Well, in that moment you want to break the cycle of your thinking. You want to change the direction of the outcome. You can't do that by doing and thinking what you always have. You must reevaluate. See how it actually feels and ask, "does it align with what I want?" Saying "thank you" STOPS THE AUTOMATIC-NESS of your response. That is what change is, my friend. That is how we manifest.

SHIFT

As I was practicing getting familiar with my body's physical reactions to my thoughts, what I would do is get familiar with how my body physically responds to stress. For me, it is in the stomach and then my whole body feels tight and closed off. I can identify it easily, as I've been practicing for so long. Because I now mostly feel calm and charged and clear I immediately notice when my body responds in a negative way. It speaks to me.

So I was in the salon with a great hair client. She told me that she had just started a Bollywood class at the Pilates studio not far from the salon, and invited me to join her for a class.

I still pause when I think of that moment... I was over 100lbs heavier than I had ever been and was in the midst of a very serious depression. The last thing I could conceive was bouncing around in a Bollywood class at a Pilates studio. That sounded like an actual nightmare I'm sure I had.

But she was a really great client and I wanted to support her so I agreed to meet her. This was certainly because I was practicing at that time being open to new experiences and becoming aware of any fear that came up.

Oh my goodness, I had a lot of fear. Triggered by what I was learning, I created a rule that was this: if I wouldn't be in any direct physical harm, I'd have to just do it—face the fear and experience it. I had to get to the other side of it. And here, my client gave me that opportunity so I agreed.

I remember it was a 6pm class because I changed at the salon and headed over to the Pilates studio an hour early so that I could park in the front and see when she arrived.

Why? Because I was terrified to go in alone. I had also discovered this fear: I was terrified to go into a public place by myself. I had never been alone to know it, and now I was, and

I was terrified to make a mistake or look like a jerk. The fact that it was a place of fitness and I was going to be the big girl I used to see at the classes I took when I was younger, thin and so naive, paralyzed me with shame and fear.

So I sat there in my car waiting. Someone arrived and went in. My heart began to pump faster because I was hoping to get in there first so that I could get a spot in the very back of the class. I felt the fear escalate.

5:30 came and she still wasn't there. I began to panic as people continued to go inside the studio. And when I say people, I mean people who have obviously been practicing Pilates, and some kind of healthy life style. I sat in my car honestly wanting to leave. I could have very easily just left, grabbed a pizza and some wings and hit the couch, but I stayed. I remember thinking, "Do I want to stay inside this box or expand?"

At 5:58 my body got out of the car and as I faced my fear my spirit expanded.

I only vaguely remember actually walking in. When I opened the door I heard my name as a kind woman greeted me and brought me into the room for the class.

It was just as I feared. The class was filled with beautiful, fit looking people and there was one mat empty—right in front. Let me be clear, I was right in front of all these people and right in front of the mirror looking back at me.

Before I had the chance to throw up or start crying, the instructor brought me to this mat. As I sat down she leaned in and told me something I will never forget.

She said, "Don't look at anyone in here. This moment is for you. I will guide you through the whole thing. Just breathe."

So I did.

I focused on her and I breathed. Then the class was over. I did it. I did it. I did it!

I was high from that class. I was high from that whole

experience. It was so ridiculous that when my client eventually showed, I stayed for her Bollywood class too.

I changed that day. I let go of a big fear. It still pops up every now and again to see if I'm really over it, and usually I am.

I have named this stage the **One Foot In/One Foot In Syndrome.** It's when things that were, get confused with what is becoming, and vice versa. It's when you are focused on what you desire and you practice that but things are still currently like they were. You have one foot in what was, and one foot moving into that new life or situation you desire. Here is where you may feel conflict and frustration. How long you spend in this stage depends on how you move your thoughts while you're here. We manifest what we practice.

Staying swept up in confusion and feeling overwhelmed will manifest more confusion and overwhelmed feelings. When you catch yourself in it and you want things to change, try to align with WHAT YOU DESIRE instead of what feels automatic. I remember a significant example of this stage from the early years of my practice.

CLIENT STORY

I had a client that was practicing becoming aware of her physical responses to things in her life. I had been teaching her about overcoming the **One Foot In/One Foot In Syndrome.** She was on alert, always checking in to see how her body felt so that she could become more aware of the thoughts that were out of alignment with what she desired. She was picking up momentum in the direction of the life she was choosing.

She described a time in her life where she was struggling. One day she said she was taking a shower. She mentioned that she rarely showered at that time because she was in such a depression. Just moments after turning on the water she heard a banging on the bathroom door. A voice yelled, "5 minutes!!! Don't use all of my water!!" It was the voice of her husband. At this point their relationship was toxic—filled with unmet expectations on both sides which resulted in ignoring each other or yelling and fighting on a regular basis.

As she stood in the shower, not even yet completely wet, she felt the rage race from her toes all the way up her body like fire. She felt a wave of fury about to shoot out of her mouth. She wanted to scream, "What the F#ck is wrong with you???!! I haven't even gotten wet yet and I haven't showered in three days!!! Let me wash my f#cking ass!!!!!!"

But she didn't. She felt that fire and identified it immediately as an old response. It was what once was. It was the thing that no longer belonged. It didn't align with the harmony and love and peace that she desired. So she didn't yell. She stopped. She caught it. She became aware and stopped.

She knew that the next step was to think of something good. She wasn't really prepared, so it seemed difficult in that moment. She wanted to scream. So she stood there for a moment and tried. Nothing good came to mind. So she sat down in the shower, trying to think of something good, but nothing. Determined as she was to redirect this moment, she turned off the water, grabbed a towel and sat on the toilet trying. She could hear him walking heavily up and down the hallway. It was intimidating, but she knew that was just HIS pattern too. So she tried harder and then it came.

On the toilet in her towel she thought, "Maybe one day when he's gone we will all laugh about how stringent he was with the water." She imagined her family all together at a holiday like Thanksgiving and they were all sharing stories about his water issues. And it worked. By that time she wasn't angry anymore. She had successfully navigated herself through the **One Foot In/One Foot In Syndrome**. She broke that pattern of behavior. She used her part of that experience to better align herself with how she wanted to be. No judgment. No fighting.

But...

He was still pacing the hallway ready to fight. She could feel his anger through the walls. But she wasn't angry anymore so what could she do?

Become aware of the FEELING

Decide if it is in alignment with what you desire or NOT

If it is NOT what you want to be feeling, think of something to generate that desired feeling.

DO SOMETHING DIFFERENT. Do something more in alignment with what you want.

She had to do something different. When she heard him coming down the hallway, this time she opened the door. He turned around ready to fight and the she hugged him.

She said when she hugged him he was stiff, ready to fight but that as she hugged him his whole body dropped a bit and softened. The fight in him left.

She stood there for the longest second and thought, "Oh

my God, now what??" and ran down the hall into her room and closed the door. She heard him through the door, standing there in the hallway for a moment. She said it was like he had no idea what had just happened. Then he slowly walked down the hallway into another room.

It was over. No fighting. No hurtful words. A broken pattern. She did it. She allowed herself to be how she desired regardless of what was. She was creating a new pattern.

She was manifesting.

Sometimes while we begin a new path, the people and things in our lives begin shifting. In this **One Foot In/One Foot In** stage this becomes evident as some of the things and relationships around you adjust as you better align with what you practice. Sometimes this feels challenging. Its like some evidence says, "what are you doing? Thats not who you are!" or, "You can't do that because of x, y, z..."

As I was just starting to come out of my dark time, I was heavy into the study of my certifications and working at the salon. Someone I admire told me that I was being irresponsible. They told me that I needed to stop what I was doing, go back to college to finish my degree and get a normal job so that I could support my daughter. They told me no one would take me seriously because I didn't have my Ph.D. or that I had ever even finished my very long college career.

They told me no one would take me seriously.

They said I didn't have the right education.

They said I was being a bad mother.

I suppose this was one of those moments that proved to me that what I was practicing worked. Once upon a time I would have fought with them. I would have tried to convince them that they were wrong, and that I was right. But it wasn't about right or wrong for me anymore. All I could see in front of me was a good person that wanted the most secure and direct path to the success they knew for me. But their vision and mine were different. There was no way they could have understood it at that time. They had no idea what I had been exposed to, and how it affected me. I wasn't even sure yet, but I WAS sure that it was becoming my purpose, my reason for being here, and I was excited by all what was to come.

Three months after this conversation I was still working in the salon and splitting my time with an amazing Doctor and his patients. I would be called in to help with pain management, mostly. The Doctor was surprised and very happy with the speedy results he saw in his patient's recovery while seeing me. One day as I walked through his office, he pulled me aside and asked if I thought I could help in surgery. He was interested in lowering the amount of anesthesia needed during surgery especially for those who were allergic. That afternoon I left the salon, and drove down the street to the surgery center. As they walked me through the pre-surgery procedures, I got into my scrubs and took a deep breath. It was happening. They said no one would take me seriously but I was about to walk into an operating room and perform hypnosis on a woman having surgery.

A few minutes later we were walking down the hallway. It was one of those moments that you see in astronaut movies—when the group of them are all walking together, slowly in a group in their space suits. That was me, with the surgeon, the anesthesiologist and all of the others I can't name, in our blue scrubs, masks—the whole thing. It was awesome. I actually remember thinking I wish someone was there to take a picture because it was so remarkable.

They told me no one would take me seriously.

They said I didn't have the right education.

They said I was being a bad mother.

Sometimes as we evolve, as we become, the things around us get shaken up. Some of those things fall away and some of them restructure. They shift and evolve with us. This is why getting clear is so important. It allows you to really get in touch with that "knowing" part of you inside. That thing that screams "YES!!! THIS IS SOOOO AMAZING!!!!" Once that voice is clear, it doesn't matter what obstacle you come across. The energy of that is so strong that it helps stay in alignment with it, instead of with that other thing—the thing that prevents it or excuses it away.

REFLECTIONS

1. What have you always wanted to do, or be good at? What prevented that from happening?

_____

_____

_____

_____

_____

_____

_____

2. What do you believe about yourself that prevents you from having what you want or being how you want to be?

_____

_____

_____

_____

_____

_____

_____

3. Where do you feel your stress? When you hear bad news, do you feel it in your head, your chest or your stomach? Maybe you feel it in your shoulders or your jaw. Identify where you feel it and what it feels like and then give it a color.

_____

_____

_____

_____

_____

_____

_____

_____

4. What makes you smile? Be very specific. DO NOT answer with "my children," or "my spouse," or "my pet." These things may sometimes NOT make you happy. Think of a specific memory, dream, or experience that makes you smile and write it here.

_____

_____

_____

_____

_____

_____

_____

_____

$$\bigwedge$$

CHAPTER FOUR

being STUCK vs. being FLUID mindset

Imagine yourself standing up to your shoulders in water.
Imagine yourself moving in the water.
Imagine yourself standing up to your shoulders in cement.
Imagine yourself moving in the cement.

Different experience? Imagine that represents how you move through your day. Are you stuck in your old truths? Are you stuck in what once was? Are you stuck in expectations? What keeps playing in your head that you wish would stop?

When new opportunities, ideas or experiences present themselves, how do you handle it? Does your first response sound something like, "I don't like change." Or maybe, "Why can't everything just stay the way it is?"

When you are exposed to new information, do you see it as a threat? Or are you more able to expand and adjust as you desire?

Letting go is a big part of the practice. Letting go of the things that no longer serve you, and letting go of anything that you are stuck in. As I learn about energy, I have come to understand why this is so important.

We are Energy. We are made of cells. Down to our smallest part, we are cells. We can see them under a microscope. When you see them you will see that the live cells vibrate. Studies have shown that what we expose our cells to actually affects how they behave. That means us. What we expose ourselves to, actually affects how we behave. Even our thoughts affect how our cells behave.

SHIFT

I learned about Dr Emoto and his work in the movie, "What the Bleep Do We Know?" I was so intrigued by what I was exposed to, that I felt a strong desire to know more. His experiments on water were highlighted in one part of the movie. I remember the scene very well. It was in a train station—underground. There was a woman talking as she stood in front of some images. The images taken were of water crystals. Some of them were beautiful, some not so much.

The woman in the train station was explaining how Dr. Emoto took water samples from the Fujiwara Dam. One was a straight sample when it was crystallized; it was chaotic and rough. He took another sample from the same water and had it blessed by a Buddhist monk. The crystal was beautiful.

Then there were pictures of distilled water. Those samples had words printed and taped onto the bottles. The bottles were left out overnight. The untouched water was an angular crystal. The bottles that had words like "chi of love," "Thank you," "You make me sick," "I hate you." The difference in the crystals was amazing. All from the same water. All with a different energy, a different word… a different intent.

The thing that got me so intrigued is that WE ARE MOSTLY WATER.

My daughter and I started labeling our water bottles. At the time I would buy cases of water. We would take markers and label the bottles with whatever we wanted to fill ourselves with… we set the intention.

We called it Love Water.

And it FELT different… it tastes more refreshing and clear and delicious… and fluid, because we ARE fluid.

How does this matter when we manifest? Well, I remember learning that professional football players take ballet. I was told that they do this to keep fluid. When they are rigid and tight, they suffer more injury. When they can remain fluid they can navigate more easily, avoiding injury.

This is true while manifesting. We often try to be the one that "knows" whatever the topic is. Whatever we know is deemed right—by ourselves. "Knowing" often keeps us stuck. This makes expanding difficult because if you believe you know all you need and still haven't achieved what you desire, than there must be something else—something you don't know yet. The truth is, that for whatever we think we know, there is a good chance something may have changed about it, or to it, or around it… There is ALWAYS something new.

I once took a Still Life drawing class. We would set our easels up in a circle around the display our teacher would have made for the day. Usually there would be a pile of stuff like candles, fruit, a wine bottle, maybe a glass sitting on a stool in the center. Once we got set up we could begin drawing what we saw in front of us. With my charcoal in hand I would diligently begin creating the image I studied in front of me.

Halfway through the class, one day, I moved my easel. As I set up on the other side of the display I was suddenly stopped in my tracks.

What I had been drawing wasn't even visible from where I now stood. From this side of the room, I was able to see fruit and flowers that I never even knew existed based on what I had been studying just moments prior.

But it was the same display. Nothing changed except my position. When I allowed myself to not be stuck where I was, when I changed how I was looking at it, that thing changed.

As you begin shifting your thoughts you may find yourself going through "difficult" moments. As we move away from what is familiar, and closer to what we desire, there has to be a point of letting go.

If your arms are filled with baggage how can you grab hold of what you desire?

And how long have you been holding those bags?

Do you even need what's in them anymore?

Letting go allows you to shift your thoughts from what is not possible or, seemingly too difficult, to possible. It removes the weight and negative feeling attached to what we do. It allows us to more clearly see what we want and how to achieve it.

At this point of manifesting or shifting your life, things begin to change. That can feel frightening because the timing is not usually convenient, or the circumstances may be uncomfortable. What I have learned is that when we desire change we must let it happen. We must let go so that the things in our life can begin to change. At this point, letting go is so extremely helpful because without the extra stress and burden you can move through the experience feeling lighter and better... which will lead you to lighter and better... ;)

Imagine right now you had a pile of black circle stickers. Each one represents everything you know. You can imagine putting them on a wall. You may feel like there are so many, that you know so much. But what if you turned off the light and saw that there are red circles EVERYWHERE and that they represented all of the truths you just don't know yet. Amazing.

And if that is hard to grasp here's another... My daughter

is 12. She is one of the most amazing humans I know, honestly. She does however believe she knows things that, because of my experience and age I know different. I asked her what life would be like if I still believed everything I thought I knew at 12. Imagine that. Rarely in life do we think we don't know; we struggle to know our whole lives. Letting go and being open to learning everything you can about everything you can—or at least what interests or pulls you in—that is where the magic lives! That is how we feel fulfilled and satisfied. That is how we learn and grow.

When you think of the phrase "let go" it may evoke a wide array of feelings. As we evolve and progress through this lifetime we are constantly changing. We are not as we were when we were 2 years old, or when we were 5 years old. We are not as we were when we where becoming a teenager, or when we were recovering from our teen years. I am no longer as I was in my 20's or my 30's. In my 40's, I have a very wonderful understanding that every single day offers change. Every single day matters. It matters because it is what is giving your tomorrow shape.

Up to this point in your life, everything is because of all of the things that have happened. All of the things you expected, and all of the things you didn't, all of the things you tried to avoid and didn't, all of the things you worked for and missed, all of the things you worked for and achieved—all of it matters.

When we don't practice being fluid or open, it becomes difficult to accept change. If you haven't checked in with yourself, you could very well be operating on an old belief system or a stale idea that is no longer in alignment with what you desire now.

When a stressful situation arises, how do you proceed? Where do you feel it? How do you react? Remember Neo from The Matrix? There's a scene where he has learned about his powers and as he is getting shot at he—in what appears to be slow motion—leans backwards and the bullets fly by him. He doesn't get shot. He is so fluid that he bypasses that whole situation.

How about walking out of the ocean? Ever try it? Ever try walking out of the ocean and one of those waves takes you down and you get swirled up in it? I have. I remember feeling like I was in a washing machine. I was pulled right in, hit the ground hard, the water was so chaotic and the pressure of it all was very scary. When I got out I was gasping for air and my body hurt all over.

I have since learned how to exit the ocean without being pulled into the chaos, and it can't be done by being rigid. I must be fluid. Just like everyday life, as things come at you—you can stand strong and unwavering in your thoughts and beliefs, or you can be open to aligning with what works best for you now. You see, you have been learning and growing. How can you be the same? You can ride the wave, you don't have to get sucked up in it. Breathe. Ride the wave.

REFLECTIONS

1. What do you fear?

_____

_____

_____

_____

_____

_____

_____

_____

2. What are your most common phrases? What are the things you say most? (ex. I'm always late, I cant ever lose weight, I will never find love, Life is just hard, I hate people)

_____

_____

_____

_____

_____

_____

_____

_____

3. Become aware of your physical reaction to stress. Do you cry? Yell? Retreat? Distract yourself? Where do you feel it in your body?

_____

_____

_____

_____

_____

4. What are you ready to let go of and what would that space leave room for?

_____

_____

_____

_____

_____

5. Create a list of power words/phrases. Write them and say them all day everyday. (ex. Thank you. You're doing it! I am calm. I am clear.)

_____

_____

_____

_____

_____

$\bigwedge$

CHAPTER FIVE
the BODY vs. SPIRIT mindset

It wasn't until my late 30's that I really began to form a new understanding of these concepts—body and spirit. Most of my life, emphasis was on mostly physical things: my body, my clothes, my car, my home, my relationships, even my friends and pets and vacations. It was all based on the physicalness of that thing, and I derived value based on what each thing was. Let's take me, for example. When I thought of myself, I thought of myself in terms of height and weight, hair color and style. Considering 24 years of my professional career was in the beauty industry, there was an absolute focus on the outward beauty, the physicalness of who we are.

I grew up in a Roman Catholic household. I learned about God from that perspective. My family went to church every week, prayed to the saints and made sure not to eat meat on Fridays during Lent. In college I took a "Comparative Religions" course. What I remember most from that class is that one of our projects involved going to several religious services. They had to be services that we were not familiar with. It was so eye opening for me. I remember the slight differences. For example, in one church people stood, when in another church people would sit. Some of the prayers seemed the same but the words were slightly

LIMITLESS

different. I heard the difference. It felt different to me. Some made me fear God. Most reminded me that I am a humble servant filled with sin. It opened me up to sharing the experience of others in that capacity.

As I began learning hypnosis and about the law of attraction I was still working in the salon. There was a hairdresser that worked in the station next to me. Every time she heard me talking about hypnosis she would interrupt me and tell me that it "goes against her religion" and that it was "devil's work." I had heard this before. I understood that when people say that, it just showed me that they don't really know about it. I would explain that, in fact, it was simply how to use your brain. "God gave you that brain" I would say, "Don't you want to know how to use it the best way possible?"

Around that same time another woman in the salon introduced me to Wayne Dyer. He was also a teacher who spoke about the Law of Attraction and how to attract the things you want into your life. I remember thinking he was too religious. He said the word, "God" a lot. To me, what I was studying had nothing to do with religion—it wasn't God. It had to do with my brain. I just wanted to know how it worked and how to work it so I could feel my best, and do my best. I didn't need to bring God into it.

And so my practice evolved.

When I began my hypnosis practice I would talk to a potential client and learn what was wrong. I would hang up and research that thing. Then I would write a hypnotic script, call them in, and read it to them. It proved to be super effective. Eventually I had hundreds of these scripts I had researched and written so when a client would call I would instinctively pick 3 of the already written scripts and low and behold! I always picked right, and the client would get exactly what they needed.

The day came that I began to wonder, after guiding so many

people into beautiful subconscious experiences, what would happen if I went to that place in our minds but didn't guide through it?

What would I find?

SHIFT

A friend of mine is an amazing yoga teacher. I remembered that at the end of her class she does a 5 minute relaxation/cool down. I knew that would be the perfect place to experiment with my curiosity because regardless of what I found I felt confident I'd be woken up after only 5 minutes.

When the time came, class was ending. We were each lying on our mats and my friend, Heather, began guiding the class through the relaxation. I, however, took myself right into a deep hypnotic state while keeping my thoughts open.

I laid there with my eyes closed and my body completely relaxed. "Open. Open. Open." I said to myself.

Nothing.

"Open. Open. Open. Open…"

Then something happened.

I saw what looked like dried ice or smoke around the perimeter of my body. It seemed to be coming from the floor. It was so curious, visually swaying, back and forth very hypnotically—like a wave. I remember thinking in my head, "What in the world?" And as I watched the 'smoke' it came up from the floor and began to climb my body, up along my sides and then BAM! Before I knew what was happening I was standing on my stomach looking down at myself laying on my mat.

I saw everything in that room while my body lay on the floor completely relaxed. I saw the other ladies on their mats, I saw my friend at the front of the room. I saw me. And then I freaked out.

On my stomach I began yelling, "Holy Shit!! I am on my stomach! How is this possible?"

Before I could even think of an answer I heard a voice. It was a voice I hadn't heard in several years and it was a voice that I thought I forgot. Until I heard it.

The voice said, "Yes Amy. We are all connected. I am connected to you; you are connected to your body and your body is connected to everything here." And there on my stomach swaying in the smoke right next to me was my grandmother, Doris Mahalick. I couldn't believe my eyes. I couldn't believe what was happening, and yet it was all so clear and so certain.

Then Heather woke us up.

I have never been the same.

I grew up Catholic. I dabbled in different religions as an adult. None of what I had learned before prepared me for what I discovered on that day. Nothing since that day has ever been the same.

In session, I often ask what a clients' thoughts on death are. It's my experience that although we talk about it in many ways— suicide, murder, sickness, loss, bereavement, stress, statistics—we rarely think about what happens after. When I ask people what they think happens when our bodies expire, they are often at a loss for words. Some mention an idea of heaven. Some mention an idea of reincarnation. Some mention an energy that lingers and helps people or figures things out. I really have NO judgment at all on what they think. What is important to me is that they understand the strength of their belief.

Here's why: if you believe in any way that there is something that happens after our bodies expire, that means you must, by default, acknowledge a part of you that is not physical. Call it a spirit, or a soul, or energy, it doesn't matter. There is a part of you that lives on BEYOND YOUR PHYSICAL BODY.

Go ahead and let that digest. Its a big one.

It even caused me to revisit Wayne Dyer because my experience with God expanded that day. My understanding of many things shifted in that moment. What do you do with this information? For me, it supports what my grandmother told me on my stomach that day. We are all connected. Maybe you've heard that before. Maybe you understand it a little differently now. That thing that lives in you and moves on when your body is gone, that thing is yours. Perhaps it is the gift we have all been waiting on. Here it is, it turns out it's been with you the whole time.

So I began to understand that our energy, or non-physical part, plays a role in connecting. You probably already know that without ever having really thought about it. You know how you know if someone is in a good or bad mood when they walk into a room? How? Because you feel their energy. We emit what we feel. We leave an imprint of that as we move through our days. People FEEL US. Or perhaps they don't... Depends on what you are feeling, I suppose.

A friend of mine was a teacher that had been out of work for a couple of years. She was frustrated and getting used to interviewing and not getting a position she wanted. One day she told me that she had an interview at a school where another friend of mine worked. I was excited for her. I even told my friend that another friend was coming in for an interview and that she was extremely qualified.

She did great in the interview and was called back for another one. It was between her and another woman, a very young woman fresh out of school. My friend was confident that she was much more qualified and hopeful for the position.

She didn't get the job. I asked my friend at the school if she could find out what happened. She told me that the principal simply said this woman had better energy. He didn't care about the qualifications and years of experience as much as how he felt around her and how he thought that would translate into a classroom. It was her energy.

I happened to be obsessed with learning about energy during this time. I remember coming to understand that we radiate what we feel. For me, I imagined it looked like some sort of tutu, like an energy tutu. Everyone wears one. You're wearing one right now. It looks like how you feel. Some, for example, are flowing and blue, some are sharp and pointy metal. Some of them are soft and bubbly, some more rigid, like cement. It became an exercise to pick what energy I wanted to wear when I woke up in the morning. I would start my day deciding how to FEEL. Then I would imagine what that looked like as a tutu. Ridiculous, maybe. Effective? Oh, yes. I would look to see other peoples tutus throughout my day. It was quite fun.

So I practiced filling myself with positive energy. I eliminated most of the negative input in my life, cleaned up my Facebook wall (kept only the positive posters), stopped watching most of what I would watch on TV (too violent or scary), and let go of some relationships (that didn't support my evolution). I added more positive input into my day—everything I listened to (mostly audio books from teachers of some sort), watched (lots of quantum physics) and heard (all the conversations I surrounded myself with).

I practiced filling myself with light.

I practiced pushing out darkness by strengthening my light.

And then I practiced its effectiveness.

SHIFT

Saturday morning in my local ShopRite was the busiest day of the week, in my opinion. I usually avoided that time to do my food shopping, but one Saturday morning during the time of my learning, I was heading there right at what I thought would be the busiest time of day. I wasn't there to buy anything. I was there to have a great pool of energy to work with.

So at the end of one of the aisles I would pause and imagine a hole open on the top of my head. A beautiful violet/white light would shoot down from above, in through this hole and down through my head, my neck, my chest... through my whole body. I would allow myself to feel its brilliance filling my body. As it did, it pushed out all darkness until I was so filled with light that I could imagine actually shooting it out of every pore in my skin.

Then I would slowly walk down the aisle.

One by one people would stop and smile at me. I didn't say anything. I didn't do anything except walk and radiate light—like sunbeams. Every single person stopped to smile, and it was packed. People were crowded and reaching and squeezing past each other but they each stopped and smiled at me as I shined light all over them.

In the next aisle I tried the reverse. I stood at the end of the aisle and closed that hole I imagined at the top of my head. I felt my energy close up. It stopped radiating from me and I headed down the crowded aisle.

I was immediately shocked as I felt the energy of each person I passed. I felt things like frustration, overwhelming-ness, tiredness. It made me feel sad. There was no light. There were no smiles, except for the occasional polite one. I felt beat up by the time I got to the end.

I was surprised how I could have such completely different experiences at the very same place. So I did it again... once with my light shining brightly and one with that light cut off.

That day I began teaching people how to feel the light inside of them. That light that feels so good. That light that feels like confidence and peace and joy and happiness, like love. It is that light that can overpower any darkness. I know this from personal experience and from professional experience.

So what do you do with something so special? How do you celebrate and care for this thing that is so magnificent?

Let's assume that up until this moment you haven't been very nice to yourself. Perhaps you have believed all of those things about you that hold you back and make you feel not special enough, or pretty enough, or good enough, or smart enough. Those things that keep you feeling dark. Perhaps, like an abusive adult, you speak to yourself in a way that makes you feel small and sad and fearful. Imagine your spirit taking those hits. Like an adult yelling at and abusing an innocent child. That is what it is like, right?

But now you know what you are doing. You are aware of this other part of you, your light. As you begin caring for and loving it you will begin seeing amazing transformations in your life.

REFLECTIONS

1. What do you believe happens when your physical body expires? How does this effect your daily experience? (ex. Are you fearful of going to hell? Do you think you are coming back in another body? Do you get another chance or is it game over?)

_____

_____

_____

_____

_____

_____

_____

_____

2. What do you think of other people? Why?

_____

_____

_____

_____

_____

_____

_____

_____

3. Without fear, insecurity, suspicion, jealousy or frustration how would your relationships change? Why?

_____

_____

_____

_____

_____

_____

_____

4. If you just met a group of people and had some time to spend with them, what do you WISH they said about you after? How would you like to be described? List 5 words. (ex. smart, confident, kind, empathetic, loving, productive...)

_____

_____

_____

_____

_____

_____

_____

CHAPTER SIX

the PROBLEM FINDER vs. PROBLEM SOLVER mindset

Albert Einstein said, "Education is not the learning of facts, but the training of the mind to think."

Problems are a part of this experience. Depending on how much you have been practicing what's in this book, your view on what it means may have changed.

MERRIAM-Webster's Definition:

PROBLEM

1 a : a question raised for inquiry, consideration, or solution b : a proposition in mathematics or physics stating something to be done

2 a : an intricate unsettled question b : a source of perplexity, distress, or vexation c : difficulty in understanding or accepting

Do these definitions excite you? What I see is that a problem is an opportunity to evolve beyond what you currently know. It could be something that stretches you and helps you figure something new out. It's something that requires your attention and openness for a new opportunity.

Very often I have clients call me all heated up because there is some kind of problem at work or at home. We are programmed to handle problems. You have been practicing your whole life.

Do you avoid problems? Fight with them? Tell everyone about them? Do you get sick? Do you take medications to help with the stress caused by problems? Do you look for problems? Do you find them everywhere?

SHIFT

Bob Proctor, one of the teachers I studied from The Secret, provided me with a very simple and profound formula that changed my life. This is it. Write it down. Meditate on it. Talk about it. Practice it. Test it. I have found it to be always viable. It works for every single thing in your life.

Here it is:

Thoughts = Feelings = Action/Inaction = Results

Every thought creates in you a feeling. That feeling prompts you to behave a certain way, and that is what gives you the results or experience you are now having. To me, that means that the results are based on what we THINK, not on what things are, or are not. That means circumstances don't matter. That means if you want something, practice THINKING about it as you WANT it to be not as it is. Think beyond what is.

For example: Love. Money. Confidence. Work. How are they showing up in your life? Does how you think about them match how they are? Crumby? Sad? Not enough? We learn to strive for things. We learn that when we achieve those things, we should feel a certain way, life should be a certain way, but its not. Life can only be what you believe it is. If you believe you will never have enough money, it may be difficult for you to finally acknowledge one day that you do in fact have more than enough. If you want love so badly, but always affirm that no one loves you, guess what? Clean out those negative truths. If they aren't in alignment with what you want, consider them VOID. Affirmations and guided visualization are very helpful for this.

A problem is seen as an obstacle that we have a tendency to deflect and defend. But what about solving the problem? There are unlimited possibilities out there so a solution (short or long term) is possible. You may just have to spend more time, or do things you don't love, or maybe even something that you fear.

Letting problems stop you and your evolution is socially acceptable. Often times friends and family will try to "protect" you from the problems you may face in the world. You do not need protection. You are a problem solver and once you realize that, you will watch things change around you.

I once had a amazing opportunity to do a study in a middle school located, in what was considered at the time, a progressive public school. One month before state testing began in the school, select students would have the chance to put their heads on their desk with the lights off, close their eyes and listen to one of my audio links. The link I made for the study was one that would allow the student listening to let go of any fear, worry or insecurity. It directed their thoughts to all of the time and work they have put into being a successful student. It reminded them that the answers they would need on the test would surface in their thoughts as soon as they needed them. It played for 10 minutes. When it was over the teacher would turn the lights back on and continue with class.

I remember coming in right after the study began. The kids had already started their daily listening. I was able to watch it happen, and it still gives me the tingles when I think of looking through the classroom window and seeing the class listening to me guiding them through the experience.

When I was introduced to the class they didn't believe it was me on the recording. Then I said, "Just close your eyes and relax..." They went nuts. They immediately recognized my voice and knew it was me.

Walking down the hallway I was stopped to be introduced to one of the other teachers who was also playing this link to her class. She said, with a twisted face, and sharp tone, "so you're going to come in here and brainwash these children?"

She sounded mean and accusing with her words as she actually glared at me. Then without hesitation or filter I replied, "Yes, but I am helping put some good stuff in there to undo some of the negative stuff they have already been brainwashed into thinking."

Do you look for the problem, or do you seek a solution? As we have already discussed, problems happen. Staying stuck on the problem, or using it as an excuse or reason to stay in the problem is, well, problematic itself.

Problems aren't always bad. They usually appear disguised that way. But you are limitless. You are able to find solutions to so many things. There are so many resources. We have access to so many things today. Use it. Use it all. See it all. Learn it all... This will help you solve problems even quicker and easier. And as you do, you will be more comfortable moving through problems.

This is happening FOR you, and not TO you.

That is a great shift for problem solving. Once I began seeing the significance in each moment it became difficult to ignore that there was something in each moment meant for me to use to evolve. There are limitless interpretations of each moment. We can attach what we know, or be open to understanding the parts as they come to be. It changes the picture a bit, provides a better understanding. It allows you to move more in alignment with how you want to be as opposed to how you don't. It puts you more in control over the direction you manifest, whether you are aware of it or not.

When you begin using a problem-solving mindset,

problems become an opportunity. You can be stopped or stalled or distracted by them, or be inspired to move past them. Your desire to do the latter will create amazing ripples that make the time you spend in that uncomfortable spot less uncomfortable.

Do you know problem makers? Complainers? I'd bet yes.

Do you know a great problem solver? Someone that doesn't seem to get thrown off their game and keeps moving forward? Me too. It's you. It's you after practicing the mindset of a problem-solver.

Often we get caught up in other people's chaos. Heres a great example of why you shouldn't.

You are just getting to work.

As you step into the elevator you trip.

The water you are holding shoots out from your hand and splashes on 3 people standing there.

One person, a person you recognize says, "OMG! are you ok? You are so silly!"

The other person, an older woman says, "Whew! Its so hot in here! Thank you."

The third person, a man in an expensive suit yells, "What the F is wrong with you? You are an idiot!"

So my question is this: Who is right? Are you silly, helpful or an idiot?

They were all right. To each person, you were what they believed you to be. Each person believed what they believed as truth. It is their truth. It is right to them.

The answer to the question "which person is right?" is that it doesn't matter. They do not define you. You define you.

We all interpret things differently. You could never know all of the reasons why any person believes or "knows" what they do. How can any other person share your exact experiences? Why would we assume any one person is acting a certain way because of what WE believe?

We often get caught up trying to defend ourselves or our

decisions. We may get judged or accused wrongly. You may offend people or hurt them unintentionally. You cannot be responsible for how people receive you. All you can do is what is good and right with good intent. Then be strong and confident on that design.

As a problem solver you can't get too caught up in the chaos that may present itself around you. Stop defending. Stop trying so hard to prove or make it "right." Begin opening to a solution. Make that a part of your thought. Make it a part of your language. Stay focused on solving the problems. You are quite limitless, so no need to doubt that you can do this.

CLIENT STORY

I was helping a woman from New York. She was a high level executive, powerful, and very success driven. She came to see me wanting to learn how to adjust some things to manifest the love she desired. What we discovered quickly into our session is that what she desired so deeply from a man are the things she had gotten into a habit of doing—she would pick the restaurant and make the reservations. She would offer to pay. She would text and call. Often they wouldn't. She felt confused. She was giving everything she wanted and wasn't getting it in return.

The problem is that she was in the way. She craved for a man to take charge, but she had a hard time letting go of the take charge position. How could he do these things for her if she was beating him to the punch?

She was creating the problem. She was fearful of it not happening, so she took that role. That prevented her from having what she desired.

Once she recognized this, she was able to move out of the way, let go of the control so that someone else could take over for her, as she desired.

This changed everything for her. People approached her differently. Men began surfacing, and they were men that didn't need her to take care of them. She adjusted so that she could receive what she desires. She moved from making the problem, to solving the problem, and we all can do it. We just have to notice what needs to be adjusted.

Often we are part of the problem, or are contributing in some way, but are unaware of it. Just like that client, I still have old programmed stuff pop up every now and again. When it does, it catches me off guard. It stops me in my tracks with a physical feeling of insecurity and fear and doubt. I can usually trace it back to some ugly experience in my past, and when I do it becomes a little easier to re-frame.

Our reactions are often programmed by things we may not be aware of. This is problematic if you are wanting a new outcome to an old problem. We can get stuck here allowing ourselves to believe other ugly truths that may be in direct conflict with that thing you desire. Ugly truths sound like: "life is just difficult," "nothing changes," "I can't," "I already tried," "it wont work."

These things, and thoughts like them, limit you. They keep you held back. They drain the light out of you, take you off your path, or create feelings of stagnation and hopelessness.

Sometimes reactions like anger are programmed. I'm certain that what makes you angry does so for a good reason. That has nothing to do with it. Its not about right or wrong. We are manifesting. What we do now affects what shows up tomorrow... Are you looking for anger? Anger is a reaction that is rarely rewarded by what you want. The question is: what do you want? Do you want security? Resolution? Information? Love? Help? Joy? Freedom? Money? Success? How does anger play a role in that? DOES it play a role? Can you be in alignment with that thing you desire while being angry? No. You can not, unless you desire anger, which I highly doubt.

For me, jealously was a reaction I learned through years of unhealthy relationships. I never realized how many things could trigger that emotion in me. It would take over my body and my thoughts in an instant. They would bring me right back to those past events, trying to prove to me that I should feel that way. I have come to understand we all have a thing, a reaction, that no longer serves us in a good way.

Becoming aware of this allows you to become a problem solver. No judgment needed. No fighting. Just get back in alignment with what you desire. Get back to practicing what matters NOW. Remind yourself that you are no longer where you were, you are evolving, growing, and can react more in alignment with what you wish for.

I recently had a client call me from work. She was "losing her mind" (her words) because there was a compliance woman monitoring her every move. This made it very difficult for her to do her job. She spent most of her days being yelled at, trying to defend herself, and combating emails that would be sent throughout the company regarding things that she said were not true.

I reminded her that she has been practicing being that version of herself she desires—calm, professional and knowledgeable. I explained that an opportunity has been presented for her. Can she continue her practice regardless of circumstance?

Practicing a positive mindset is easy when things are going well. It's in times of difficulty that we get deep though—those difficult times force us to get down into our ugly. What happens then is up to us, and is directly connected to what you have been practicing.

Do you acknowledge that ugly, that thing that is no longer in alignment with what you want? Can you dismiss it as what was? Or do you give yourself permission to stay there longer, to believe it more, to keep it real?

Here's a quick tip: when you feel yourself reacting in a way that is different than what you desire, stop. Just by acknowledging that it is what you use to think and is no longer valid, you have changed the program. You have already changed the response. You did it just by being aware.

From there you can begin practicing that new response.

What it looks like and sounds like, what you look like and sound like. Let it be your guide. Its like you get to decide before it happens, so when it happens you know just what to do—in a way that is closer to what you want.

This really is the dress rehearsal. What are you practicing? That is what will show up for you, I promise.

During my transition from darkness I remember seeing myself for the first time in hypnosis.

In class for one of my certifications our teacher took turns putting each of us in and then out of hypnosis. He wanted us to see what it looked like and what it felt like. When it was my turn I couldn't believe what happened.

I was in a room. I seemed to be coming into the room from above, almost like I was flying or gliding in from the back. It seemed like a conference room—like at a hotel. There were chairs lined up and an aisle down the middle. The seats were filled. The lights were dim and everyones attention was on a woman speaking in front of a podium under the lights in front of this audience. I floated from the back towards the front, noticing how everyone was listening so intently to the speaker. As I got closer still I discovered that the speaker was me—but a very different version of me. She looked amazing. She was in a white pant suit, sharp and crisp. She had beautiful flowing shiny hair and a French manicure pedicure combo. Her skin was glowing... She looked confident and happy. She was so beautiful I began to cry.

I tried to hear what she was talking about because at that time I hadn't spoken in front of a group like that. I had no idea what I could be speaking about but it looked so good. The whole thing looked so damn good.

I woke up feeling reborn. I was just coming out of my depression. I had no idea what I was doing, but I just saw something that looked like I was doing it right, so right. I looked radiant, happy, confident, so damn good.

I would go back to that place in my mind often, gathering

more information each time. I would collect the pieces and begin literally putting the pieces together. My first switch? My shoes. I hadn't worn heels since my depression and was living in sweats and flip flops for two years. In my vision I saw myself looking so good I knew that eventually I would be wearing heels again—that is what I wanted to manifest. I didn't know what to talk about. I had to grow my hair. I had to lose weight. I had to get an audience. I had to get my skin good, find a suit and ... you get it. If I wanted to make that happen I had to get comfortable with all the parts. The only part at that time I could practice was my shoes. I went to Payless and bought the highest heels I could find. I brought those bad boys home and would wear them in my apartment. I had to practice wearing *heals* again... it was that simple. Piece by piece.

I started doing a session like that on my friends. I decided that since I got myself into a bad spot I should be fired from being in charge of me. My new boss? That version of me in the white suit. She obviously knew what to do. I want to feel like her look like her... she is me. So I do what I can to be in alignment with who she is—my successful self.

There was a period of time a friend and I would meet at the local track at 5am before we had to get the kids up and get off to work. We would walk a mile or two. It felt good. I loved it as much as I hated it.

One morning as we pulled up and parked the car, the sky opened up and it started pouring rain. My reaction of course was, "Woohoo! I get an extra hour of sleep! I'm going home!" Then I remembered I wasn't the boss anymore. I looked at my friend. I told her we had to check in with our bosses. It took only a second for us to get out of the car laughing our asses off. We walked around that track laughing like crazy people in the pouring rain I had no choice though, my future self said, "You're here to walk, Amy. Get your ass out of the car and walk." So I did.

REFLECTIONS

1. When something unpleasant unexpectedly shows up in your life, what is your response?

_____

_____

_____

_____

_____

_____

_____

2. What is the biggest problem or obstacle that you have overcome so far in your life? Use as much detail as possible.

_____

_____

_____

_____

_____

_____

_____

3. Have you given yourself credit for all of the obstacles you have overcome so far? Do that now. Do that here:

I am so proud of myself for…

_____

_____

_____

_____

_____

_____

_____

_____

4. Think about the top 3 things that bother you in your daily life. Using the formula
THOUGHTS = FEELINGS = ACTION/INACTION = RESULT, determine what thoughts would provide you with a best result.

_____

_____

_____

_____

_____

_____

_____

_____

CHAPTER SEVEN

what you should know

Sometimes, even after great practice, some of those negative old thoughts will surface, trigger and ripple through your body. Remind yourself that they are foreign thoughts now. Your body won't experience them as often, so when they arise, let it be an immediate attention-getter. I immediately remind myself that is what I use to think and pour gratitude all over it... I'm so grateful for _____. Let your brain know that what was is no longer; you are changing. You are manifesting.

Remember that you have been programming yourself your whole life. Now that you can actively participate in your experience, become aware that your body responds to thoughts. Become familiar with what negative thoughts do to your body. Does your jaw clench? Do your shoulders get tight? Does your stomach hurt? Does your chest feel heavy? When this happens during a stressful time, let it be an alarm for you indicating that what you are thinking is **WRONG**. Your body is physically rejecting it. Now, if you have these feelings, I strongly suggest you get to the doctor. On your way there, change your thoughts. I have seen blood pressure greatly reduced, and pain dissolved. I have seen the physical reactions to stress completely stop, leaving the participant more calm and clear.

You are not weak or strong or smart or dumb or carefree or

stressed out—you are only whatever you tap into and use. You and the world around you are a reflection of what you have chosen to believe. You can adjust whatever you'd like along the way. We are limitless, far more capable of whatever limits may hold you back. Decide what you want first, then practice feeling it.

Practice seeing every person and where they are and what they do as nothing more than the result of their thoughts have led them to at this time. Just like you. Stop taking things personally. Begin to understand that every single person is doing the very best they can at every moment, even the not-so-good ones. Just like you. Relax. Stay in alignment. You are manifesting.

There are some things you can begin doing today that will help you feel better quickly. Practicing them regularly will allow that feeling to build momentum, strength and speed.

1. Stand in front of a full length mirror. Thank your body for caring for you after all of these years and after all you have put it through. Thank your spirit for not giving up. Make peace between the two.

2. Create a playlist of teachings—information about getting better and doing better and how. Listen in the car, eating, walking, doing the laundry. Set your energy by directing your thoughts and increasing the amount of "good stuff" you fill yourself with.

3. Fill your thoughts with, "Thank you." Your thoughts are running automatically. When you want to change something, finding gratitude is ridiculously helpful. It allows you to feel good. It allows you to overcome and move through whatever you are trying to get past. It will also lead you to positive people, experiences and opportunities. Just keep saying "thank you" in your head.

REFLECTIONS

1. List every single thing you are grateful for. Dig deep. I mean
EVERYTHING.

_____

_____

_____

_____

_____

_____

_____

_____

2. List all of the qualities you like about yourself. (Go wild here.
What do you do well? What do people compl ment you on?
What do you enjoy?)

_____

_____

_____

_____

_____

_____

_____

_____

3. Close your eyes and do the following:
Take a big deep breath.
Hold it for 5 seconds.
As you exhale slowly, drop your shoulders.
very good…now do it again.
Take a big deep breath.
Hold it for 5 seconds.
As you exhale slowly, drop your shoulders and say "thank you."
repeat 5 times.

4. Think of the people and places that (used to) bother you.
List them and what you don't like about them.

_____

_____

_____

_____

_____

5. Take the people and places you listed in question
#4 and list them again here. Now find something
good about them. It's ok to be creative, but remember
Thoughts = Feelings = Action/Inaction = Result, so do your
part here.

_____

_____

_____

_____

_____

TRUE STORIES
Amy

In every traditional sense of the word, I had a highly successful life before I began to work with Amy and learn about manifesting. I had a new husband, a new home, and an exciting career as an executive. I just couldn't stop grinding my teeth. Literally.

I'd taken up yoga and meditation to learn to relax but was experiencing limited progress, and at my yoga teacher's recommendation, I set up a consultation with Amy Arvary to experiment with hypnosis as a potential solution to help me unclench my jaw.

The first thing I learned was how much my unconscious beliefs and assumptions were coloring the way I looked at current situations. For example, I felt very frustrated and lonely being in a new town where I'd moved so that my new husband could live close to his young children. My own child had just graduated high school in suburban New Jersey, and for most of his life, I'd been planning to move to New York City when he left the nest. I love the energy, diversity, and creativity of a big city and always pictured myself as an "empty nester" in New York, exploring and enjoying my passion for the performing arts, particularly comedy.

But my step-children lived in the opposite direction, so I had to make a tough choice. The choice was even tougher because both my husband and I travel extensively for work, and I spent many nights alone in the mountains, many hours stuck in traffic to or from the airport, wondering if I had short-changed myself and given up on my passions and dreams for the sake of a new family who didn't even get it, or get me.

When I started working with Amy, she took me through visualizations letting go of the past and picturing a dream future. Looking at the past, I was amazed to gradually uncover how many of my feelings of being an outsider ran deep and went back to a difficult experience in middle school, when my family moved to a new town where I did not fit in and was bullied and ostracized for two years. I had so many negative assumptions I was unaware of that were stopping me from embracing my new family, community and home.

Beyond letting go of these past feelings, I gained a new sense of excitement and possibility by visualizing the kinds of experiences and feelings I wanted for the future. Suddenly I began seeing the beauty in nature, the warmth and friendliness of the people around me, and the reality that creativity and performing arts are everywhere. I took up hiking, created a garden, made new friends and started what has proven to be a never-ending series of creative interior design projects with my husband. I also realized New York City is not so far away that I can't make it in at least once or twice a month – it was my own all-or-nothing thinking that had made it seem like I'd given it all up when in fact, possibilities are everywhere, and we always have access to the best qualities of ourselves.

The impact on my career has been even more dramatic. I had climbed fairly high on the corporate ladder, all with a view to putting my son through college. I knew the stress and intensity levels were taking a toll on my overall health (and my teeth!) but I enjoyed the satisfaction of overcoming challenges, the prestige of a glamorous title, and the confidence that comes from knowing I am capable of leading large teams through complex challenges. I thought I just needed to get better at managing stress and developing a thick skin. In my early life, I'd wanted to be an entertainer but a fatally flawed singing voice seemed like an insurmountable roadblock. So I took the more practical route of starting with my "day job," figuring I'd find a way to work in performing arts as a hobby along the way. In my early career, I did lots of teaching and presenting – things that naturally gave me a platform to exercise my love of entertaining and inspiring groups of people. As I rose through the ranks, I spent much less time in front of an audience, and more time in meetings and behind spreadsheets. Because I was in Marketing, I got to be involved in many things that relate to entertainment and creativity. For example, I would make a business case for a large-scale event, put together the right team to make it happen, and be there to see all the pieces coming together – but that is not the same thing as being on stage myself and seeing people's faces light up with insights and laughter and hope for the future because of something I just said.

As I practiced visualizing the future, images like those kept popping up. Me in a room full of people, laughing. Me on stage with lights in my eyes, feeling the energy of the audience. It became increasingly clear that my current job was not my "forever destination" and I started consciously letting go of the present, letting go of my assumptions about my future career path, and visualizing myself using my natural drive, humor and passion to help people change their lives. Before too long, my company was sold, and I found myself with a severance package and an opportunity to go back into corporate education. Luck being very much on my side, I was able to take a summer off to recover from the burnout of my last job and spend extra time on my health and happiness so I could go into my next one with a renewed attitude and not get into the downward spiral of chronic stress.

The first thing I did was take a comedy workshop in the city. I started doing stand-up at open mics as well as practicing jokes on my friends. I kicked off a creative project with friends in California where we published a comedy cookbook. It ended up taking two years to get from concept to published book. Investing that kind of time and energy just for laughter and fun would've been unthinkable to me before. When I returned to work full time, it only took a couple of months before I became "too busy" to do stand-up on a weekly or monthly basis, but instead of taking that old "all or nothing" approach, I fit in where I could. Working on the cookbook, doing occasional open mics in the city, watching more comedy and working on my material are all things I still managed to squeeze in.

All that said, in many ways I was still frustrated with my work life. Although my team was out there in front of audiences delivering workshops, I still spent the majority of my own day in back-to-back meetings, behind spreadsheets, and rarely making anyone laugh. I still experienced stress-related health challenges, though to a lesser degree, and I still felt drained at the end of most work days. But I continued on the journey trusting things would unfold as they are meant to, letting go of old negative assumptions and self-limiting beliefs, and visualizing the future. I've found the journey happens in a series of constant baby steps, and sometimes they all suddenly add up.

After two years of these baby steps and many candid conversations with my boss, my friends, and myself, the perfect opportunity arose. Right now, my job is to travel the world delivering workshops that help leaders and individuals bring out the unique best in themselves and others. I get to use my favorite talents and practice getting better at telling stories and jokes. I get to see faces light up every day. When my boss presented this new opportunity to me, she told me she kept thinking about the quote from the Shawshank Redemption, that some birds are too beautiful and brightly colored to be kept in a cage and that I belong out on the road in front of people. Only two weeks before she said these words to me, I'd evolved my old college tattoo. It had been a faded bird just hanging out solo on my ribs, and now it was a bird in flight coming out of a beautiful art deco floral design. This is a great example of what manifesting means to me. Letting go of old assumptions and negative beliefs; listening to the unique voice within that reconnects you with who you really are and has the wisdom to understand how being exactly who you are will bring you exactly where you belong; and embracing the journey with gratitude and curiosity.

The practice of manifesting has unlocked new levels of joy, peace, happiness and fulfillment in my every day life, and I am only about four years into this lifelong journey. It is with deepest gratitude that I share this story and wish you every happiness and much love and laughter in your own journey.

What I learned about manifesting: be receptive. Let go of my need to understand and control. Embrace the universe and trust that things will unfold as they should. Just because I don't understand something doesn't mean it's negative. That's an interpretation. Withholding judgment and replacing that with a sense of thankfulness and curiosity is a whole different state of mind –a freer, happier state. Knowing I can't control many things gives me a sense of freedom and relief –I am just one person in the universe. Looking inside for what the universe has given me—the unique perspectives, abilities, fears, likes and dislikes— manifesting for me means being and becoming more of who I am naturally set up to be vs. fighting against the grain to become someone I think I should be.

I have moved from "daydreams" to realities. A sample of something I've seen that has come true: I had a picture of the walls of my kitchen melting away like in *"Where the Wild Things Are."* Fast forward, my kitchen has been redesigned and the landscaping outdoors all feels like part of the same fun, luscious, peaceful scene.

Donna

This journey of mine began back in 2011. I was at the lowest of my low. I was scared, hurt, broke and lonely….I made the decision to get a divorce. I had no children and my husband at the time said to me he would be miserable for the rest of his life with me, but he wouldn't get divorced. Then and there I made the decision to not live miserably for the rest of our lives. I didn't want him to live like that and I sure didn't either. If you have been through a divorce you can imagine the heart ache and courage it took to do this… However in the process I learned a lot about myself and how I wanted to live and love for my life. I took two days to cry, literally I lay in bed and cried. I can't even explain the difference I felt after this. I felt like I could finally move on, I had to put on my big girl panties and go to work and create the life I really wanted. So I did!!!!

I began reading about meditation learning about chakras and dabbling in essential oils and of course manifesting. I was all about love, I wanted everyone and everything around me to be surrounded with love. I would have a love bracelet, and a love scarf, that I would wear every day. I was figuring out what it meant to love yourself. This was a beautiful experience for me, during this time I was able to spend time with dear friends, and family, and was realizing that I was manifesting this life of love.

So as I go about my journey, about a month into it, I go on a blind date, to not only meet the love of my life, but he also has LOVE tattooed on him! Talk about manifesting a life of love! I was so nervous I couldn't eat, and was shaking trying to take a sip of my drink.(Me thinking in my head: it had really happened, I manifested this man and found love!) I did this, I created a life of love and I wasn't sure if this was truly the man of my dreams, (being that it was a first date and I still couldn't help but be a little skeptical…) LOL, the last part is BS, he was and still is the man of my dreams. I am completely blessed and honored to call this man my husband every day!

So when someone says to you, "you will know when you find your true love," you will KNOW!

When people say if you want something you have to make it happen, MAKE it happen!

You are the creator of your destiny, do it and do it well!
XOXOXO

Jen

I was 15 when I had my daughter. At that time my focus was being able to feed her and put clothes on her back. I found a job in a local pizzeria and worked every second I wasn't with her.

There was no thinking about my future at that time in my life. The life I was living was hard. My only focus was on making enough money to care for my daughter.

1996 I meet a guy who I thought was my best friend. Shortly after, we bought a pizzeria together. I did everything from serving tables to making pizza, cooking and scrubbing floors.

In 2000 we married although I knew our relationship wasn't the kind I once dreamed of. He was mentally and physically abusive. I was scared every day until the day came for me flee that life and I did.

My self-worth was shattered. We divorced in 2003.

A friend suggested I come work with her as a closing agent for mortgage companies. I was so nervous because it was so different than what I was familiar with. For all of my life I worked in jeans and a tee shirt in the pizzeria. I learned how to dress professionally. I bought a suit and that friend trained me to be a closer for a title agency.

I studied everything I could and became good. So good that mortgage companies and law firms were requesting me to do their closings. I was manifesting what I desired before I ever even knew it.

I became aware of the Law of Attraction around 2007. Watching it made me realize my life is what I make it, what I create it to be. I learned that what I believe in my thoughts I can actually do. I learned that I can be anything I choose to be. I began to practice.

I started with *The Secret*. It introduced me to all kinds of new ideas and gave me good techniques to practice.

A few years later I found out that the friend that brought me into the title agency world was practicing hypnotherapy. We reconnected and began sessions immediately.

This put me in a whole new ball game. It was all home runs from there. I could have the life I thought was only a dream. It was actually my reality just waiting for me to believe it.

I would and could be as successful as I chose to be. I became less fearful and less distracted. I became confident. And as I did, I became even more successful.

Today I own my own Closing Agency. I employ amazingly like-minded professionals. I have built wonderful relationships, helped thousands of people and married the love of my life.

I manifest without trying now. My practice has become my life and all I had to do is trust that there was more for me—and shatter the fear that kept me from it.

Lenny

It's unbelievable the amount of mental power we have that we don't even know about. Our minds are so complex that as humans we have only a small clue about the capabilities that it holds. However, figuring out these capabilities can change the way we live and interact with world around us. In fact, the more you become aware of the power your mind has the more connected you become with the world around you. I found this to be true when I was introduced to manifestation.

Going into my senior year I found myself to have intense amounts of anxiety before football games. I knew the plays, I had the strength, but the worry and fear that would arise before I stepped on to the field was unbearable. I would wait all week for our scrimmage or game and the second it was go time I would want to hand in my pads and quit just to escape this unnecessary fear that consumed me. This troubled me so much. I had waited my entire football career to have a starting position on the Varsity team. Now here I was with my dream position, the size and strength I needed to dominate, but a mind that was holding me back. I was at a complete loss and had no clue what to do. This was when I had my first session with Amy.

My mom and Amy were great friends and I had met Amy many times before. Though I had a general idea of what she did for work I had never actually worked with her myself before. My sister would see Amy about once every other week for a session to deal with her anxiety. I remember so clearly seeing rapid positive changes in her mood and the way she carried herself through the day. Whatever she was doing with Amy was clearly making a difference and I knew that having a session with her would likely result in similar changes in myself. Though all I wanted or expected from my time with Amy was help with my anxiety what

I ended up getting from our sessions was so much more. It was knowledge and power that would change my life forever.

My session with Amy began with simple conversation. We talked about school, about life, and of course about what was going on with me, and football. As we looked deeper into my issue with football, we began to break down the different parts of my anxiety and assess what the root of the problem was. After our talk concluded things got interesting.

Amy explained to me that she would now be giving me a personal meditation using the information from our conversation. I sat back into the chair and put on the headphones, both nervous and excited about what this experience would be like. The meditation began with simple relaxation and breathing exercises. These were used to calm me and open my mind to a state of plasticity so that everything I heard during my meditation would not only register in my mind but alter it in a way that fit my ideal mindset.

The meditation had a lot to do with envisioning the outcome and lifestyle that I wanted. I was challenged to picture myself on the football field feeling the way that I desired. Feeling confident, strong and unstoppable. I pictured myself entering the field on game day with no stress and no mental limitation holding me back from success. And honestly, just thinking about this felt good. After the meditation concluded, we talked about my experiences and perceptions they aroused during this time. I explained to Amy how I had pictured myself living the athletic life that I desired and how good it felt to see myself so well off. In addition to this, we talked about how easily obtainable that lifestyle was and how continuing to picture that lifestyle will eventually result in me living it. This, she explained, was manifesting.

I've come to learn a lot about manifesting and to this day I can say it's changed my life so much for the better. I had spent nearly two weeks since I had my session with Amy practicing manifestation. I would meditate when I woke up, before bed, or any other time throughout the day that I had a free fifteen minutes to dedicate to my cause. As I continued envisioning my ideal situation, a life where I would step onto the football field feeling powerful and excited as opposed to weak and anxious, I began to see noticeable improvements in my mindset. I began practicing harder, enjoying myself on the field more than before, and having an overall boost of confidence in the way that I played football. However, this was just during practice and I wouldn't know how effective my first attempt at manifestation was until game day.

When I woke up on game day, I was feeling different than usual. Instead of waking up with my normal feeling of stress in anticipation for my day, I actually felt ready. I appreciated this change in the way I felt and became very excited that my meditation practices were potentially working. I wouldn't know exactly how well they were working though until I stepped onto the field. When I walked onto the field for the first game of my senior year, my energy was unlike anything I had ever experienced before. I could feel the power surging through my body. I could feel the exploding emotion of excitement to start the game and show the other team what I was made of. What I could not feel was the anxiety. I felt as if I were cured from a horrible disease. All the time dedicated to re-teaching my mind how to react to the football environment had paid off and now I was living a life so much better than I could have hoped. I was ready to make something of myself with no mental drawbacks this time. Nothing could stop me. I was living the life that I had manifested.

Manifesting is possible for anyone. All it takes is an open mind and persistence. With manifesting, you have the power to control your thoughts and emotions and expel anything that is not useful to you. In addition to this, manifesting gives you the power to make any dream a reality. I realized in my time working with Amy that by envisioning your desired future you subconsciously begin to act in a way that will assist in the acquisition of this future. You start to change small things and make different decisions than you normally would because your mind is now working towards this desired outcome. And this can be used for anything! It can be used for grades, for work ethic, for breaking or starting new habits. It can be used for changing the way you see and understand yourself. Any time you have something you want to change or achieve, manifesting can help you do it.

In the year and a half that I've been aware of the power of manifesting, I have used manifesting to become an animal on the football field, to completely flip the way I felt about my body image, to get into Penn State, to improve my speaking skills and honestly the list goes on for too long to type everything. Once you obtain this power and begin to master it your mind becomes unstoppable and there is no limit to what you can achieve. With manifesting, I've become a better person and with it so can anyone else too.

Jessalyn

To manifest. What does this mean? The word defined, means an event, action, or object that clearly shows or embodies something, especially a theory or an abstract idea.

To me, the concept of manifestation is when you believe in your greater power to call forth the visions you hold within your most powerful mind, creating it as your reality. In our society, so often when we see a person living a life that seems to have been designed for their happiness, we may feel as though we are not lucky enough, or we are not fortunate enough. Maybe they had it easier, thus creating this beauty surrounding them daily. We cannot have that, and so on. We continually tell ourselves why we can't live to our greatest potential, or our greatest desires.

Therefore as we continue to allow our brains to carry those thoughts into the universe, alas, that is EXACTLY what we end up living. Those destructive thoughts create our lives to our own detriment, yet we made it that way. Thoughts are one of the most powerful aspects of our brain. They control our actions and our ability to line our path to our present, and our future, however we think it will be.

In my young life, my greatest manifestation to date happened to me in the summer of 2009. From 2000 to 2009 I lived in a pit of darkness. By design I had created this life of anger, artificial love, superficial relationships, addiction, infidelity, spousal abuse, and unsettling unhappiness. My self-esteem was inoperative, at best. My ability to live was lead only by a mother's love for her children, the tendrils of joy I felt found in their eyes, and this spark sustained me as each 24-hour period renewed itself. During this period of time I learned to understand that what I was feeling, what I was living, felt foreign to me. I had surrounded myself with individuals who behaved in such a manner that I felt my body shrinking away, in hope I might become so small I would be invisible. Yet I still participated. I had my place in that world and although it felt strange, as if I were an alien placed in a world I didn't belong in, that is what I knew. It was my normal. My childrens' normal.

January 2009. A pivotal month in my manifestation. It was here that I watched **The Secret,** a movie that assists you in seeing how significantly your thoughts create your reality. My sister soul-mate, Amy Arvary, had gently been placing this movie into our conversations, and eventually it's physical presence in my home, for months at that point. She saw my life, and the struggles I lived with daily, her love for me apparent always. She saw me. She saw the me I couldn't see. With patience and unparalleled love, Amy persisted in her goal to help me realize the potential residing within my broken soul. This transition sparked a part of my brain which released a wave of understanding as to the concept of living. Life is not meant to be lived in a state of sadness and negativity. Life is a promise of purpose, a period of time you are gifted with, and it is up to you to design your minutes. Your days. Your years. We, as humans, are given the potential to grow within ourselves, body and mind, on a daily basis, and so often we choose to ignore our intuition and stay on the hamster wheel placed before us.

Fear is one of the driving factors that frames our reasons for staying in a situation which we know is not ideal. You will hear an individual state other excuses, some valid, others not. Yet it is fear which holds us back from breaking through the mold we have created. It is of the unknown and the known. It is deliberately awakening the intrinsic consequences which have the potential to destroy you.

Fear—in the same—is beautiful. To embrace fear is to look into the unknown and scream at the top of your lungs "I CAN do this!!!" and maintain the courage of knowing that nothing, and no one, will stop you. Because you will not allow it.

And that, my friends, is what I did. I often explain my experience to people who ask "how did you get out?" in a relatively simple form. Over the course of a few months I felt myself coming back. My courage, my soul, my brave spirit. It was in this period of time my eyes were opened on a larger scale to the many facets of my life that were detrimental to the health and growth of my impressionable children, especially at such young ages. It was during this time that I prepared for my departure from this life, and as my strength progressed, I explain the process this way: it was as if everyday I continued to hit this impenetrable brick wall. As my desire to leave this repugnant life gained momentum, so did the obstacles standing in my way. Every single day I would continue to hit that brick wall, desperately seeking a path over, a tunnel under. Anything that could hurtle me forward towards this new life I so fiercely desired, and had been planning for.

And that is where fear came to play. In your life there are certain moments you will forever see vividly in your mind's eye. It is in those moments that you are intensely aware of your actions, and how those brief periods of decision have the ability to change the course of your life in the most cataclysmic way. As I stood in my home, this massive figure poised before me, full of rage and vehement wrath, spewing the words which put my fragile mortality at the forefront of my mind. It was not my end. My vision was swimming with the faces of my children. Of all the experiences I still wanted to participate in. Of the life I could see waiting for me.

I broke through that fucking wall.

64,512 days of darkness led me to a lifetime of light.

Manifestation. What does it mean to me? It means that you need to take charge of your life. The power resides in you to create your path as you want it to be. As I sit here, 9 years later, in my incredibly happy home full of sunshine, love and peacefulness, continuing to manifest all that I desire into my life, I ask you to think about all the obstacles you believe are holding you back from living the life you desire. Write them down. Scream them out. Now tear them up. YOU are the only obstacle holding you back from every single thing you want to achieve. As a single mother of 3 young children, with $20 to her name, I took a leap into the unknown. I had absolutely no idea how I was going to survive, how I was going to make even the tiniest part of creating this new life work. But I took a flying leap onto that proverbial first step, the staircase invisible and non-existent. It was terrifying. It was exhilarating.

If you are not living the life you desire. If you are not living to your full potential. If you are existing as an entity in a world where you are walking blindly through...is that really living? Trust your intuition, break your wall, and take the leap into the beauty of a life created for you, by you.

Jessica

I was 12 when my father died in the World Trade Center on September 11, 2001. I was in 7th grade at school when my class mates and I were told to go to the auditorium. I remember being in the auditorium when my principal was explaining what had happen to the World Trade Center. I knew right then, and my dad was a hero.

Up to that point, my days consisted of pretty normal stuff. I was like most 7th graders. I was into riding my bike and I loved to roller blade. I enjoyed being with my family. But on September 11th all of that changed.

I knew it wasn't my fault, and I couldn't help. I felt as if my world was taken from me. I had a lot of feelings. What killed the most was I knew could never go back and change what had happened to me.

The following two years were foggy. I was filled with a sadness that was taking over. It was difficult to understand the pain and confusion and sadness involved in such an experience. I didn't just lose my dad. My father was killed in a terrorist attack.

How does one prepare for that? I was 12. My days were suddenly filled with tears and anger. I had to deal with these feelings I had never felt before. I have two younger brothers who had the same feelings I did. Except I was the oldest, so I felt so guilty that I had the most time with our dad. I felt bad for my brothers because I remembered dad a little bit more than they did. I watched my family for years drown themselves in tears. And what could I do?

In 2003 I was diagnosed with Post-Traumatic Stress Disorder. From that moment my suffering had a name. Severe depression and anxiety controlled me and helped me feel more and more hopeless. My condition controlled me. I ended up in a very bad depression. I was in and out of hospitals for a few years. My condition was in complete control of my life. I thought that this is who I am now and there is nothing I can do to change it. I know my dad would want me to be happy. I was trying to be happy but my condition had complete control.

15 years into my suffering, I was sick of suffering and sick of pretending. I was at rock bottom I tried everything. Nothing helped me. Until I became a medical cannabis patient for the state of New Jersey. It changed my life dramatically. It alleviated some of that pain. It cleared and calmed some of the anxiety. About that same time my cousin introduced me to Amy. My cousin heard me say I wanted nothing more then to be happy and to not pretend anymore. She told me to try one session with Amy. She said Amy helped her find that, and bet that she'd help me too. My first session with Amy was the best thing that happened to me. After that first session, I felt a ton of weight off my shoulders. I began practicing everything Amy taught me till the next time I saw her. I did my affirmations in the morning and meditation at night. Within a week I noticed my depression cloud was moving away faster then it ever had. I finally realized that I was wrong all these years—I am not stuck like this. Amy guided me, and showed me how to control my condition to the point where I realized that I can heal.

It is 2018. Just one year ago I had no idea what was ahead of me. I began the practice of opening myself to opportunities and ignored any negative thinking that came. I began seeing myself more confident and more ready. I found strength in all of the things I once thought broke me.

It became clear to me that I can help others experiencing PTSD and more with medical cannabis. In January, I left my family, my fiancé and friends, and traveled across the country to take the plunge into this new life. That was only a few months ago.

I recently graduated with a certificate of achievement from Oaksterdam in CA. Momentum has picked up now. Manifesting has become the life I live. I have found my place, my purpose. I have learned to love myself and remain open to all of the gifts that are constantly showing up. Don't stop. It's in you.

Tara

I was very fortunate growing up. I had a mom who was very much before her time and began teaching me about mediation, hypnosis and sending my intentions out into the universe. She would put my brother and me to sleep with relaxation techniques, telling us to envision people, places, events, and to feel energy and light around us to help us, guide us and heal us. It was the foundation of a skill set that would change me in ways I can't even explain.

Growing up, as with most younger siblings, I idolized my brother. He was the coolest person EVER! He was everything I wanted to be and more. He was my protector. I knew no matter what, my brother would always defend me and keep me safe. As we grew older we got even closer. Don't get me wrong, we still fought as all siblings do, but in the end the love we had for each other was deep, very deep and very pure.

When he went off to college I was a regular there, visiting him and his Frat brothers. My college friends and I would drive 2 hours each way to go hang out with them often. I always knew no matter what we did or where we went we were safe as long as we were out with him.

In our early 20's we would meet weekly to have dinner and catch up. I remember one night he said to me, "Tara, we always have to stay this close. Promise me that—that we will always be close. One day our parents will gone and we will be each other's only connection to our past." Those words have never left me. They are words I have spoken to my own children from the very beginning of their lives, that's how strongly those words hit me. I have thought of them many times over the years and how lucky I was to have such a special bond with my brother.

My brother secretly struggled with depression. Because of our bond he would share some really dark, scary thoughts he had about wanting to harm himself. I never thought that he would really do anything though, after all he was the strongest person I knew. No matter what, he was always on a pedestal in my eyes.

My life is divided by a simple date. Everything before is one lifetime and everything after is another. About 2 weeks prior to this date I had a conversation with my brother. He shared with me how far down a rabbit hole he really felt he was, like he was backed into a corner and nothing he could do would change that. After more than an hour on the phone with him I felt hopeful and optimistic. I really thought I had gotten through to him a bit, I know he had heard me and I know he felt my love for him. He even texted me later that day thanking me and telling me he knew my words were the truth and he would follow my advice. The next few weeks life got busy and I didn't really speak to him much.

May 14, 2015 will forever be etched into my soul. It was a beautiful sunny warm day, easily the nicest day of the year so far. I remember sitting outside feeling the warmth of the sun hitting my face, feeling so happy. I had so much going my way, ironically it was the most content I had felt in a really long time. The evening set in and as I walked out my front door I remember feeling like spring had finally arrived and life was good. At the exact same time a few miles away my brother had set into motion a plan that would permanently alter everything. Within 90 minutes of me feeling this overwhelming peace my brother would be gone from this earthly life.

I received a phone call from my brother, I couldn't answer but he left me a voicemail. Shortly after receiving it I listened to it. I got 13 seconds into the message and I stopped listening, I knew from the way he sounded what he was planning to do. The next 45 minutes were spent frantically trying to figure out his plan, where he was and how I could stop him. Ultimately I would end up being literally 5 minutes too late. He had taken his own life. My life came to a screeching halt and everything I knew instantly ended. Time was now frozen. But I couldn't fall apart—not yet, I had to tell my mom what happened, and I had to stay strong; stay in one piece so I could give him the funeral he deserved. In my mind I needed to walk him "home."

Shortly after his funeral I had this venom that seeped into my veins, it was an anger and sadness so poisonous, and it got worse with each breath I took. Life was happening around me but I was dying. The pain was so unreal, and so unbearable. I honestly wanted to die too. I wanted to join my brother because I couldn't stand the idea of living the rest of my life without him. I would often curl up in my bed hugging his ashes, wishing God would take me. I was completely and utterly broken—broken in a way I didn't know was humanly possible, and I didn't know how to help myself. All the lessons my mom had taught me about intentions, mediation and energy were fruitless. I was simply shattered into a million billion pieces.

I had met Amy about 3 years prior to my brother's passing, in a yoga class actually. Instantly I was drawn to her, but the timing for us to truly connect wasn't perfect yet. Over the next few years Amy and I would frequently enough run into each other, and I would always feel this intense draw to her but never acted on it.

It was now July, and the venom in my veins had really taken hold, and no matter what I did try to get rid of it I couldn't. This was not what my brother wanted for me, this is not what I wanted, I had to do something. A mutual friend suggested going to see Amy professionally. Maybe she could help me, maybe she couldn't, but I had nothing to lose so I made the call.

Amy and I spoke on the phone for bit and she explained what exactly she did. Because of the exposure my mom gave me to these ideas throughout my childhood, everything she was talking about was very familiar, and I knew I needed to try this. During my very first session I told Amy every detail of the night my brother died. It was the first time I said any of it out loud. I cried, a lot. Then she told me to close my eyes, and what happened next still gives me chills, even now as I write about it.

During my very first hypnosis session she brought to me to a small cabin in the woods. The inside of the cabin was completely empty. After being inside for a few minutes she had me walk to the front of the porch of this cabin to where my brother was. I was able to feel my brother, feel his energy, feel his touch and just be with him. I was drinking up every second, deep gulping breaths, I never wanted to leave. Then he took my hand and placed it into my mother's hand and then left. I woke up from this session with tears streaming down my face, but I wasn't sad. This was the most magical experience and the sense of peace I found in this cabin would be just the beginning of my journey.

For about a year I would go to see Amy weekly, while listening to her links daily. I would look forward to my sessions with her like a drug addict needing their next fix. I even brought all 3 of my kids to Amy. I made my mom go to see her, I made my cousin go, even co-workers. I wanted to tell everyone, shout it from the highest mountain top what these sessions where doing for me. Amy wasn't just helping me navigate the darkest waters I had ever faced; she was changing everything about me. EVERYTHING.

My sessions with Amy have unlocked a part of me I never knew existed. Through all of my struggle I found a strength I never knew I had. Her hypnosis has transcended to all areas of my life, I have been able to break through professional barriers that had weighed me down for decades. I have learned to stand up for myself and speak my truth. The gifts Amy has shown me are gifts that no one can ever take away from me and the best part is, they don't just stop with me, they have affected everyone around me! The energy in my home is completely different now. My relationship with my children has always been close but is now limitless, our conversations are very different, I can't really put it into words but it is simply amazing.

Looking back on the last few years, my personal growth and evolution is undeniable. I struggle trying to find the words to express how far I have come and how my mindset has changed. When I reflect over the last few years the only thing that comes to mind is an old Japanese proverb: "when the Japanese mend broken objects, they aggrandize the damage by filling the cracks with gold." They believe that when something's suffered damage and has a history it becomes more beautiful. Amy took all of my brokenness and carefully put me back together filling my cracks with pure gold. My gratitude is boundless. Thank you, Amy.

Lorena

I met Amy around 2014. We both volunteered at the same non-profit and clicked from the moment we met. All I knew about what she did was that she worked with clients all over the country helping them cope with various issues via hypnotherapy sessions. At the time I didn't really believe that what she did really helped... to me if felt like talk therapy. Don't get me wrong, talk therapy is amazing and it definitely works to help you deal with so much of the baggage that life throws your way. The idea that what she called "guided meditation" did much of anything wasn't really something I was convinced of.

About a year after I met her I accepted her offer for a session to see what it was that she actually did. The rave reviews from everyone that worked with her were enough to have piqued my interest. That first session made me an Amy fan for life!

Yes, I know how cheesy it is to think that one session could do so much, but it honestly did.

To help you understand what it did for me, how it helped and why I'm eternally grateful to her I need to give you a brief background on who I am.

I was raised in a household with divorced parents who came to the land of possibilities from South America. My father took off for good when I was fourteen and though there were many attempts at reconciling my relationship with him, it never truly worked out. My mother tried her best to care for my younger sister and me. Unfortunately, my mother suffered from an immunological disorder that made her extremely ill pretty much all of the time. My mother also never really bothered to learn English very well and so she relied on my sister or I to do all the translating for her wherever she went.

When my father left us, he left no savings and tons of past

due bills. My mom cleaned houses for a living, so if she didn't work that day there was no income for her to bring home.

My mom was sick all the time. The kind of sick that had her in the hospital time and time again with doctors trying to figure out what was wrong.

This meant we struggled a lot to make ends meet. Someone had to step in and provide for all the essentials, so I started working at the age of fourteen. Lying about my age to get full time work allowed me to provide for my mother and younger sister. Since my mom couldn't (or wouldn't) speak English, I also had to step in as the parent for all my sister's school functions.

I was in an advanced math and science program in my high school, writer in the school paper, in the high school cheer/step squad, working full time, pretty much raising my younger sister (though she was only two years younger), and taking care of all my mother's medical needs. I don't recall the number of times we were faced with having to say goodbye to my mother because she was losing another battle with some unknown health crisis. The doctors were always amazed at how we would cope and then bounce back. The social workers were always on standby to figure out where my sister and I would go if she passed.

To say I had a lot of stress from a young age is truly an understatement.

I worked hard to finish high school at the age of 16 and started going to college at night while working full time. We didn't know my mother had an immunological disorder until I was seventeen. By then I had considered joining the military but knowing that I would not be able to care for my mom or sister while I was enlisted, and possibly deployed, terrified me more than anything.

Life has a way of balancing the good with the bad. With all the crazy thrown my way I also had some amazing things come my way. I met my husband at the young age of eighteen and we were married by the time I was twenty-one.

For more than twenty years he and I have been able to face the crazy adventures that life has thrown our way.

One of those adventures was a relocation for my husband's career shortly after my own diagnosis with a different type of immunological disorder than the one my mother had. The one I was diagnosed with was causing major physical changes, I had gained about 60 plus pounds in a very short period of time, and it was causing major mood swings.

It was a year after we had moved that I met Amy and tried her guided meditation for the first time.

I remember so clearly sitting there thinking "this will just be a quiet few minutes" but instead she opened my mind to emotions I had buried deep, deep inside me for well over twenty years!

She guided me to a house that had a massive stairwell. She told me to take the staircase down to the door at the bottom of the stairs. She said the walls down the stairwell may or may not have pictures or perhaps my favorite color on the wall. Once at the bottom the door was supposed to open up to my relaxing place. Once I walked in through the door I would feel relaxed and open to what the future might bring.

What I experienced in that moment was surreal. The staircase had photographs of memories when I felt stressed and anxious. Moments in my life when I felt overwhelmed. When I got to the door it felt heavy. Like I really needed to push that door open. I couldn't cross the threshold though. I kept looking back at the stairwell.

Amy then told me to "give myself permission to step through." I did step through and I walked out onto a beach with the sun shining down on me. I could feel the warmth of the sun on my face. I could feel myself letting go of years of stress that had been built up. It brought me to tears. When I was brought back I was surprised to feel different and to have tears on my face.

Amy asked me what I had seen and what I had felt. I started to cry again. I truly felt as if I had left the years of stress behind me.

What Amy did in that session was something that years of therapy didn't do. Don't get me wrong, talking about my experiences and my emotions was definitely helpful. Learning how to cope with not only the stress but the anger that had been building up from being forced to grow up too soon couldn't have been done without the guidance of some very good therapists that I saw in my 20's.

After that session I knew that what Amy provided was the visualization to accept things that I had not been able to do in therapy. I was able to feel the feelings of moving on to new things without having the anger and stress from years past. Therapy had provided me with the reasons why I should let go but I did not know how to actually feel those feelings of letting go.

After that one session I saw her regularly and I thought I had finally learned how to handle stress.

Yet nothing prepared me for July 2016. See, in addition to all the health issues my mother had, she also dealt with ovarian cancer and uterine cancer in her early 30's and more breast cancer scares than anyone I know. My father had colon cancer in his early 40's. Genetic testing said I was not positive for the genetic markers but the number of family members with a combination of these cancers is frightening. My mother also got Non-Hodgkin's Lymphoma and lost her second battle to it before the age of 60. I made sure to start getting early screenings for anything and everything early on to hopefully avoid health scares.

July 2016 was my fourth mammogram and breast ultrasound. I had been getting both because of the family history of fatty tissue being misread as tumors with my mother. Every single scan had been completely clear of anything. On that Wednesday in July, the technician asked why I was getting both mammogram and breast ultrasound at 36. I gave her a synopsis of the paranoia in me and how I wanted to be sure I was one step ahead of anything that might ever be. I told her how I had even talked to my husband and kids about what I would do if in fact something was ever found. This is what we chit-chatted about as she got the room ready and verified facts for the scan. Then the scan started and her facial expression changed.

They are supposed to show no emotions, right? They are supposed to not tell you anything. Yet her comment scared me, "good thing you are so proactive, early diagnosis is always the best." I got dressed and left knowing the doctor would get the report in a few days. About an hour after I left I received a phone call from the radiology department asking me to please return at my earliest convenience. The doctor wanted to redo my breast ultrasound. They also said not to bother with making an appointment, that whenever I could return I just needed to let them know I had been told to ask for a "priority appointment" and they would get me in right away.

Now I was really scared. A medical facility calling you back right away and telling you not to make an appointment???

I had felt a couple of lumps in my left breast a few weeks before the appointment. I did monthly breast exams in the shower. I had gone to see my doctor, she had checked me, and when she couldn't feel them when she did my exam she had said it could have been because of my period. Since I had my annual radiology exam coming up I disregarded them as they had been small and hard to find again.

Needless to say, with the phone call I received, and the knowledge of the missing lumps, I immediately turned around and went back to the radiology place for them to do another breast ultrasound of both breasts. This time there was another person in the room typing things into the machine. They gave me no other information nor answered any of my questions. They were no longer chatty and friendly but more somber and serious.

They sent the report to my doctor that very afternoon. My doctor called me that evening to make sure I would see her the next day. When we met the doctor told me that they had found four masses: two in each breast. One of them was very close to the skin and that was the one they feared the most. I was told that they needed to be biopsied as soon as possible and that a breast MRI would be needed to map out where they are exactly and what kind of biopsy would be needed for each.

I spent the next 10 hours in a state of numbness. My husband was trying to comfort me, yet his words weren't registering. I feared telling my kids. I didn't want to scare them, but I also didn't want to keep them in the dark. We are a family who shares everything and I didn't want to start hiding things now. I saw Amy that next morning and asked her for help.

Her session that morning led me to a beach where I was able to soak in the sun and listen to the waves. She used phrases that reinforced the message of letting things go and not jumping to conclusions. After her session, I was able to take my daughter, who was about to be a high school freshman in the fall, to lunch to explain to her what was going on. My daughter amazed me with her maturity and coined the term "boob invaders." She said we would simply need to make sure we kicked the boob invaders out. I then talked to my son, he was only going into fourth grade, and told him the same thing I told my daughter. We talk openly about boobs, period, etc in our home so he isn't afraid to discuss anything with us. His only request was for us to tell him if he needed to be scared. That if we said it would be ok he would be believe us.

Without Amy's session that morning I would not have been able to handle my talks with them with such calmness. I wouldn't have been able to focus on the next few weeks of testing and appointments. She helped me focus on the good around me instead of where my mind wanted to wander to.

The kids went to a family counselor and Amy for the next few months. I didn't want them to be scared and become afraid to ask questions. Without her my kids would have internalized their emotions, perhaps being unaware of how to feel scared without feeling overwhelmed. She helped them cope.

By this point you already can guess why Amy is so important to me. And even so the BIGGEST reason why I will never allow her to drift away from me is because her tips, sessions and recordings guided me through the scariest chapter of my life.

I opted to not have biopsies done but instead went for a double mastectomy with reconstruction. I didn't want to leave any opportunity for anything to come back after some time. I met with her while prepping for the surgery. Using her affirmations for allowing myself to focus on healing and to focus on the masses being benign. I knew I was going to have a tough road ahead of me. I had never done well with pain medication and I knew that this was going to involve a lot of pain. I asked her to focus on pain management for the weeks leading up to the surgery.

Turned out my sensitivity was an allergy to opiates, narcotics and certain muscle relaxers. No matter what they gave me to fight the nausea and the hives that I got from the medications, it was like a scene out of the Exorcist every time I took them combined with hives all over my body. After a 12-hour surgery I was bandaged up and unable to move my arms or core upper buddy without excruciating pain. I spent a few days in the hospital with the doctors trying to figure out what to give me for pain. Nothing worked. Instead I was in more pain every time I took something for the pain since that caused me to throw up and use muscles and movements that caused me pain.

I came home trying to hide the pain with Tequila. My liver was not going to be happy.

About two weeks after my double mastectomy I broke in hives across my chest, arm and back. Thinking it was yet another allergy the doctors gave me the usual run around of trying pill b after pill a didn't work. What no one thought of was that I would get the shingles. After 7 days with the rashes and pain getting worse they finally realized it was the shingles. Pain from the surgery was excruciating. Pain from the shingles was an entirely new level of torture. I was out of my mind unsure of how to manage even just a few hours without pain.

I had been using Amy to deal with stress and anxiety but not on pain management exclusively. We set aside a few sessions where I could focus on healing and not letting the pain win.

It was beyond magical! Without her recordings and sessions, I would have been incoherent every day, drunk on Tequila. Instead I survived a double mastectomy, an exchange surgery, and a total hysterectomy with just learning to how to mediate for pain.

Jennifer

As I pull on my warm sweater, open the door and step on to the balcony; I can feel a cold air rise up my body from the floor. My socks are not enough to keep my feet warm in this weather. I take a deep breath and I can smell a crisp wintery smell. I listen to the light patting of rain on the roof top adjacent to the balcony. I am grateful that this balcony allows me a moment of opportunity to breathe and enjoy this rainy/winter day. See, I am standing on this balcony because I need inspiration, focus, and direction. I am about to explain to you the powers of manifesting and how it has changed my life. This is not a small task, there is a lot to capture in just a few short paragraphs. It is true that making a daily practice of focusing my thoughts, learning to feel a connection to my heart center, staying in a place of gratitude and giving, has forever changed my life for the good and it will change yours as well.

I mean this poor Irish/Italian girl from a broken family is standing on a balcony off her master bedroom suite, overlooking an amazing piece of land, breathing in the winter, hoping that she can put into words the amazing power of manifestation. So here it goes. The story does not start here, not on my balcony, with my family, our businesses or the amazing life we have created. Instead it begins in the car with my soon-to-be husband driving us on a long road filled with miles and miles of trees. There was not a town in sight, my left hand was interlocked with his right hand. I held the directions to a place that I found by "accident" in my left hand and that is where we were headed. See, my aunt had been married a few years before our engagement and the wedding was held at a magical weekend resort in Nevada. Randy and I loved her wedding and our vision was to find our own magical venue on the east coast. This is what we were manifesting except the magical venue idea seemed a bit impractical due to our financial status.

Randy and I did not have parents to pay for our wedding. We just finished putting ourselves through college and we had many student loans coupled with the fact that we had just purchased a "fixer upper" home that we secretly laughed and referred to as the "money pit". We had a vision for that as well and it included a balcony off the master bedroom suite.

To say we were financially strapped was an understatement. We would have been lucky to afford a barbecue in our over grown weedy/wooded yard. We believed in manifesting and we identified our vision as finding a wedding venue that felt like my aunt's and allowed us to return over the years of marriage. We were engaged in June, and that winter we saved enough money to put a plow on Randy's old truck that he worked on just as much as he used. The winter was a cold snowy winter and Randy plowed day and night. He waited until spring to sleep and all of his plowing efforts had saved us some money. We were really excited that we had some money saved to go toward our wedding. We began to look for a venue. If you have ever priced a wedding in NJ you would quickly learn that wedding venues can cost you as much as a college education. I was researching this referral for an affordable wedding venue when I accidentally stumbled on the website of this magical and amazing wedding venue. I can remember when the web page opened up my heart had that very familiar feeling of "this is it."

I felt that same familiar feeling in my heart as we drove holding hands. I can remember being in the car driving up the hill, passing all the trees and noticing a sign. "There it is, make a left here." As we made the left we began to pull into the long driveway, over the bridge and up on top of the hill was the most beautiful stone building we had ever seen. Our hearts sank and we both knew that we fell in love but neither one of us said anything. We parked our car and went to the front door. What were we going to do here? We didn't make an appointment. We had no one to come and see, so we confessed to the bellhop that we didn't have an appointment but we were looking at wedding venues. He explained that it was our lucky day. They happened to be having a wedding expo on that day. He directed us to the activities. The inside of the building was just as magical as the outside. I felt reluctant to look at any of the wedding exhibits because I knew how much money we had saved and I was not sure that we could afford such a magical place. So we whisked past the venues and explored the building. We went outside on the beautiful stone porch and we strolled through the gardens, then we explored the putting greens and gazebo then we ran inside downstairs past the family game room. We found the indoor pool and marveled at its beauty. Then we saw the signs for the lookout tower. We followed the signs up the many flights of stairs down the hallway then up one more metal set of stairs and at the top was a heavy door. We opened that door and stepped out to the roof top balcony overlooking 5500 acres of pristine land. The moment was amazing and the feeling magical. Randy turned to me, grabbing my hand, and suddenly said "I cannot wait to have our anniversaries here." It was just as we had been manifesting. That week we called to inquire about having our wedding at their location. After all the decisions had been made the exact cost was the same amount we saved. On August 20, 2005, Randy and I had the most magical wedding, and we have gone back to visit Skytop Lodge every year following our wedding date. We decided to visit Skytop this past Valentine's Day and they happened to be having horse and carriage rides. As we were in the horse and carriage looking up at the building that we love so much, I knew that it was this story that I need to tell you. We are so grateful for the love and joy we experience though manifestation and I hope this story inspires you to manifest all that you desire.

Nicole

At age 20, I was diagnosed with Ulcerative Colitis. I have dedicated most of my adult life focusing on overcoming the disease through lots of trial and error. I want to give others hope that you can live the life you imagined regardless of the challenges you may face.

It was a beautiful October afternoon with that crisp fall air but still warm enough where you did not need a jacket. It was a Tuesday which was special to me because my dad always said everything good happens on a Tuesday. As I walked on to our walkway with our house keys in hand, Steve, my boyfriend at the time, said "you go in first"! I eagerly opened the red front door with my vitamin drink and phone charger in my other hand. As I turned left into the empty kitchen there sat a velvet ring box right on our blue kitchen counter. Before I could realize what was happening, Steve was on one knee proposing to me! This was one of the best days of my life. We had just bought our first home together and now we were engaged—all on a Tuesday!! Our families came over to celebrate that night and it was a truly perfect day. I did not realize it then but that day was the last day I truly smiled, laughed, and felt internal happiness for a long time.

What I did not realize was that my chronic disease, Ulcerative Colitis, was going to destroy me one day at a time in the days, weeks, and months ahead. I thought I had beaten the disease but I was so wrong. Symptoms came on very fast after we moved into our new home and began planning our wedding. I started to drop weight drastically because I could not keep anything in me, so I was not absorbing any nutrents. I became pale, lethargic, depressed, anxious, insecure, emotional, angry, frustrated, overwhelmed… the list could go on and on. I stopped going into work and started working from home because the struggle to leave the house daily was crippling.

What they do not tell you when you are battling a chronic illness is how it affects you mentally, not just physically. All the emotions I was feeling were just getting worse and worse. I was basically homebound and felt so hopeless. I did not want to look at myself in the mirror because I was so upset with how I looked. I felt like I was being punished and somehow, I deserved this. I felt alone. I forgot how to laugh, enjoy the moment, and be me. I lost me. Every single part of me.

The part that killed me the most was that before I got so sick I was always high on life. I loved being with family and friends. I loved adventures. I loved being spontaneous. I loved food. When this disease came back everything I loved stopped. I stopped seeing life as fun. It was hard...really hard. I stopped wanting to be around family and friends because I knew I was "depressing." I did not have that fire in me anymore and I truly felt unworthy. I almost punished myself and thought I deserved this sickness. I did not deserve to be happy. I used to scream out loud with my hands raised, "What did I do to deserve this"? My relationship with food was devastating. I loved cooking and eating. But then everything I put in my body was being rejected. I began to fear food. But then again, I began to fear everything. I did not know who I was anymore and it was terrifying.

I thought if I sheltered myself I would one day miraculously get better. If I hid from the world that my physical and mental symptoms would just disappear. If I just lay my weak body on my brown leather couch everything will just get better. Life will just turnaround. It will all be okay. I will be okay. But when the first year passed and I was still the same, lying on my couch barely able to pick my head up, feeling hopeless, I knew something needed to change. I needed to change but I was not sure how.

One of my favorite quotes from Oprah is, "you become what you believe." In my opinion, that so clearly explains manifesting. When I was introduced to this new way of thinking and doing my entire world changed. I will never be the same because that is how POWERFUL this practice is. Every negative feeling that I was struggling with for so long was lifted. Once I was introduced to this MAGIC my life transformation began to unfold FAST and I could not believe my eyes.

The funny part of it was that I was still battling my Ulcerative Colitis but something was happening. I did not see my disease as a curse anymore. I saw it as a blessing. I happily said, "I am grateful for every experience that has brought me to now." What? How could I believe that because for so long I looked at my chronic illness as a curse and a punishment. I even would scream out loud. "Why me?" It is truly remarkable how once you change your thoughts your life magically turns around.

I cried hard when I thought about how I saw myself. I was so underweight I could not fit in any of my clothes. I was so frail you saw my chest bone. Before this new mind shift I was told to repeat the following: "I love myself, completely." Buckets of tears poured from my eyes. I thought to myself, "How could I love myself?" but the funny thing is once I started telling my mind what I wanted it to think, it listened!!! I do LOVE myself, completely. And you know what? I am still not in remission!

Some of the things I was telling myself or believed were true just weren't. I was taught that I have the power to become whomever and whatever I want. It is all about how you see things. Handle things. React to things. I started to envision my life and how I wanted it. Who am I?

Once I stopped listening to the untrue thoughts my mind had created I could replace them with my new truths. I could walk down the aisle on our wedding day confidently. I could have the courage to book a flight to Nashville to stay with a woman for a few weeks to teach me how to heal my body. I was content the day my corporate job laid me off because I was transitioned to long term disability. All these things were happening to me once

I started envisioning and believing my worth and listening to my new truths. You may think OMG how could this girl be happy? She lost her corporate job, she is on long-term disability, and she is still not in remission from Ulcerative Colitis? The thing is all these things have been a blessing to me. I am so grateful for my journey because it has led me to where I am now. I have never been happier or more content with where I am in my life. I am taking care of myself. I have found my fire and passion again. Through all this I have found me. Someone once told me that sometimes you need struggle and failure to find your true purpose. I truly believe that through this journey I am exactly where I am meant to be.

I swear I woke up one morning and decided I wanted to help people. I absolutely love food, exercise, and connecting with people. I was given an opportunity to become an online health and fitness coach and I did not think twice! I want to inspire others to take control of their lives seeing my journey. It isn't perfect. It isn't pretty, but it is my journey. I have found my happiness again and without changing my mindset and following the Universe's "signs," I do not know where I would be right now. Manifesting was a word I had never heard of. I had no idea about the complexity and power of it. It is MAGIC. I have lived it firsthand. I have seen it. I have felt it. I have stopped in my tracks and laughed because I have seen my life transform in ways I could not have imagined. AND the only thing that I have done differently is BELIEVE. BELIEVE in myself, my worth, and my mind.

I wanted to share a post I wrote on Facebook recapping my journey and how I feel. This really explains how I felt before and how I feel now. This is what manifesting your dreams can do!!!

Close your eyes.

Think of YOURSELF!

How do you look?

How do you see yourself?
Strong?
Weak?
Lonely?
Happy?
Underweight?
Overweight?

When I did this exercise last year I saw myself weak, tired, helpless, hopeless, drained, unworthy, frail...the list can go on and on!!! I didn't feel good about myself at all. It was really hard to look at myself in the mirror or take a picture because of how I felt inside and out. When you have a chronic disease like Ulcerative Colitis it can really take a toll on so many aspects of your life.

Fast forward to now!!! I did the same exercise and you know what? I didn't look like that girl anymore! I saw myself strong, happy, hopeful, relieved...I even envisioned myself in a beautiful RED dress feeling confident. I wear a lot of red and this is why!!!! RED symbolizes my happiness and how far I have come!!! It's my reminder to never give up and to keep fighting for perfect health. It was important that I share this because I want you to know that YOU have the power to change how you see and feel about yourself. You have the POWER to change your thoughts and your life. I am PROOF!!

Kate

I am 16 years old, and I am a junior in high school. Let me just say, this has definitely been a stressful time in my life. I'm sure many of you have experienced the classic, "what are your plans for the future?" question. It is so great, isn't it? Especially when you're someone like me, who has zero clue whatsoever.

Wrong. It is not so great.

Unfortunately, it is a pretty big contributor to the whole stress thing. I am going to get real with you all for a bit. I've been a pretty stressed person for the majority of my life. Since before middle school, I have struggled with very severe anxiety. I know that I am definitely not alone in this situation, considering that this is something that so many teens and adults in the world go through. However, towards the end of middle school my anxiety had gotten to a point where it really began to cripple so many of my life experiences. I would avoid social situations, because I would never feel truly comfortable outside of my house. Branching out and trying new things was something that did not come easy at all, which was also hard to deal with.

During our younger years, I believe it is so important to experience what life has to offer, and to truly grow as a person and into an adult. My anxiety was preventing me from doing so. I hid this really well, so a lot of people who hear this about me are pretty shocked. However, it was truly a battle for me internally. Going into high school, I really wanted to make a change in my life. I wanted the mornings where I could not get out of bed to end. Most importantly, I was done taking the back seat to my stress.

I'm going to be honest, admitting that I had a problem was definitely not easy. I felt as if it made the whole situation more "real," if that makes sense. Well, I can say with zero hesitation that it was the best decision I've made. The answer to why is pretty simple; I began my journey with manifesting.

I started to meet with Amy the summer before my freshman year. I knew that my quality of life would get so much better if I figured out how to control my anxiety and how to live with it. So, my mom and I really searched for the person who would be able to help me do so. This search led us to Amy.

Meeting Amy was such a huge blessing for me, because she is not only someone I can trust, but the person who introduced me to meditation. People who are unfamiliar with the process of meditation definitely get pretty confused when I talk about it. For example, some of my friends initially believed that I would go into her office, get knocked out, and wake up doing all the things she told me would help me. Although that process sounds pretty cool (and extremely creepy), it worked a bit differently.

My visits with Amy would begin with some great talk therapy. I would let her know what was going on in my life at the time, how my anxiety was making that worse, and what I would love my future situation to look like. Then, I would close my eyes, and listen as Amy would guide me through a peaceful place and a life in which I would overcome whatever obstacle I was facing at the time. Afterwards, she would send me my recordings, and I would listen to them every morning or night, depending on when I needed them. This helped me in more ways than I can count.

Exposing my mind to a life in which I lived without stress was just what I needed in order to realize that it was possible. For awhile, my mind would constantly race with "worst case scenarios." This is a main reason why trying new things and meeting new people was so hard for me. Through working with Amy, I realized how vital it is to redirect these thoughts into something more positive. This relates to the law of attraction, and the fact that what you focus on truly expands. So, during times where I am in a dark place, I've learned that focusing on what else could go wrong would only make things darker. This is the reason why anxiety was a struggle for me for so long. Amy taught me that just a switch of my thoughts was all I needed to see actual results and changes in my life.

I am not going to lie to you, it is much easier said than done. However, this is something that I promise will work if you are willing to put in the time. When I am in a dark place in my life, all I have to do is tell myself that the one constant thing in life is the fact that everything is always changing. This is so important, because it reminds me that any struggle I am going through will pass. It is okay to feel overwhelmed. It is okay to be nervous. It is okay have doubts about yourself. But only focusing on the negatives will never lead you to feel any better.

Since my journey with Amy began, my life has made a complete 180. Before we met, even the smallest problems were hard to bear. I would think to myself, "This won't change. I am doing this wrong. I am not good enough for this." Clearly, life wasn't too peachy. Today, I am so grateful for all I have learned. I am now aware of the fact that life is such an exciting journey.

Everything that happens to me is not against me, but for me.

Dealing with my anxiety is an everyday practice. Meditation is part of my daily routine, as well as constantly shifting my thoughts into something more positive. Another huge idea that has helped me in my life is the fact that staying present is so important. We cannot change what happened yesterday, and we cannot control what happens tomorrow.

What we can do is appreciate the present moment, and all that life has to offer as it unfolds around us. I've learned to look at every single day as if it were a roller coaster ride. Sure, I don't know what to expect. Sure, there are many ups and downs, and it can be scary. But that does not mean it can't be fun and amazing when I just enjoy the ride. I am manifesting.

Notes

LIMITLESS

Notes

LIMITLESS

www.ingramcontent.com/pod-product-compliance
Lightning Source LLC
LaVergne TN
LVHW021512080426
835509LV00018B/2489